Please remember that this is a library book
and that it belongs only to ~~~
person who ~~~ is
not write ~~~ this,

I1034101

The Philosophical Foundations of Paranormal Phenomena

Harry Settanni, Ph.D.

UNIVERSITY
PRESS OF
AMERICA

Lanham • New York • London

Copyright © 1992 by
University Press of America®, Inc.
4720 Boston Way
Lanham, Maryland 20706

3 Henrietta Street
London WC2E 8LU England

Library of Congress Cataloging-in-Publication Data

Settanni, Harry, 1945–
The philosophical foundations of paranormal phenomena /
by Harry Settanni.
p.   cm.
Includes bibliographical references.
1. Parapsychology and philosophy.   I. Title.
BF1045.P5S47   1992   133'.01—dc20   92–23295 CIP

ISBN 0–8191–8867–0 (pbk. : alk. paper)

 The paper used in this publication meets the minimum requirements of
American National Standard for Information Sciences—Permanence
of Paper for Printed Library Materials, ANSI Z39.48–1984.

CONTENTS

ACKNOWLEDGMENTS

I am heavily indebted to the two institutions in which I teach: Holy Family College and St. Joseph's University. Also to my graduate and undergraduate education, enbracing St. John's University (NY), St. Joseph's University and Villanova University. Several individuals stand out: my mother; Dr. Francesca Onley, Drs. Schiavo, Moyer, Michael, Grugan, Hobaugh, McCormack, Osenlund, and Fr. Al Smith, all of Holy Family College. At St. Joseph's College, Dr. Lawrence McKinnon, a most outstanding colleague. But also, very important, Drs. Godfrey, Linehan, Jenemann and Wachterhauser. The attractive typesetting is the work of Clorinda DiDomenico of 69th Street Terminal Press, Upper Darby, PA.

PREFACE

Many investigators in the field of paranormal phenomena think that they can substantiate their claims with more impressive evidence than that which is required for the confirmation of scientific theories in many other fields. And yet paranormal phenomena does not have the same credance or widespread acceptance that many other established areas of science do. Why this dichotomy? Could it be that despite the empirical documentation for all kinds of strange happenings and events in the area of the paranormal is more than sufficient, none of this gels with our more traditional understanding of the world?

Possibly paranormal phenomena does not cohere with a more traditional, scientific understanding of the world around us, and it is perhaps these foundations which must change. No wonder some scientists are reluctant; no one wants a change in the foundations. We are accustomed to viewing the world through the framework of a very specified understanding of what we consider to be the nature of the physical world, the nature of morality, and indeed, the very nature of reality itself. It is just this traditional understanding which we may have to change if we want to accommodate the paranormal as a part of reality. In other words, the foundations of our more familiar philosophy of nature, our traditional philosophy of morality, and probably even our metaphysics, our understanding of what reality, may have to undergo sharp revision.

But the more man extends the natural range of his experience, the more he casts aside his previous molds. This is nothing more than the story of history. Already, intimations of such a new philosophy of nature, of morality and reality are manifesting themselves in rudimentary form in our contemporary culture. It is the purpose of this book to look at these new seeds, these new foundations and to awaken the consciousness of the reader to them. He may then see how the entire range of paranormal experience accommodate these new foundations.

For this purpose, the present work has been divided into three parts: Foundations, Problems, and then, Reflections. In the first part, the new foundations in the philosophy of nature or of science and in the philosophy of morality are contrasted with the old (Ch.I) and then the application of these new foundations to paranormal phenomena is revealed (Ch.II). In the second part, the author demonstrates how the same new foundations can solve certain crucial problems, which though they may seem to border on the fantastic, may nevertheless become increasingly more vital as the future proceeds. These are problems relating to whether the mind can be reduced to the brain, (Ch.III), and the problem as to whether source of our personal identity lies in the body (Ch.V). In closing, there are many reflections on the new understanding or reality which paranormal phenomena provokes. The chapters on

Dimensions (Ch.V) and Space-Time and Spinoza, (Ch.VI), respectively, raise the question of just what kind of reality space and time present to us and of how both space and time may leave us less receptive to other features of reality, namely, the psychic. In Seeds, (Ch.VII), I point out how even some ordinary elements of experience point to features of reality which may exist, beyond both space and time. In The Last Frontier, (Ch.VIII), I attempt to peek a little below the surface of our experience in the physical, spatio-temporal world and into the psyche itself, which could, in reality, be the source of space and time. In the last chapter, (Ch.IX), once again, but in new terms, the author addresses himself to what he considers to be the emerging philosophy of paranormal phenomena.

Today's reigning forms of science in established circles cannot accommodate the reality of the paranormal because this experience will not fit into its framework. But a more comprehensive science of the future, the outlines of which are sketched in this book, may yet find a true home of this exciting avenue of investigation, and it may become the focal point of future scientific research.

PART ONE

FOUNDATIONS

CHAPTER ONE

THE ETHICAL IMPACT OF TWENTETH CENTURY SCIENCE

It is a well-known adage that the twentieth century world is dominated by a scientific outlook. One might, in broad terms, refer to the philosophy of the twentieth century as the scientific world-view. Indeed, many think that the only true knowledge of the universe which is available must be obtained by rigorously following the canons of scientific research in the formulation of theories and in the confirmation of these theories in experimentation. Science is the only path to certain knowledge in the perspective of many, and this philosophy has gained pre-eminence since the beginning of the twentieth century. According to this view of the world, sometimes known as positivism, ethics and religion are not credible fields of knowledge because they are incapable of submitting their respective data to these criteria. For example, altruism, simple justice, the Natural Law, and the reciprocity of the Golden Rule are ethical ideals which are not subject to experimental confirmation in the laboratory. There is no laboratory experiment which can prove whether these ideas are for the "good" or for "evil", hence, they are cognitively meaningless. At any rate, ethical ideals can never be derived from the facts of laboratory experiment and, according to our scientific outlook, on the facts are relevant. It is impossible to derive an objecitve code of morality from the fact. The consequence of this, at least according to much that is current in our scientific world-view, is that since morality has no factual basis, it is a matter best left entirely to the private tastes of the individual, and to his whims and desires. If any ethical worldview at all can be derived from the sciences, according to this outlook, it is an ethical worldview in which individualism and subjectivity reign supreme, even to the extent of trampling upon the legitimate rights of others in the selfish desire to advance oneself. A great deal of current immorality can credibly be attributed to the increasing acceptance of the positivistic interpretation of science, and to the scientific world-view erected upon this.

If it is true that current immoralism can be traced to the positivistic world-view established upon the foundations of the physical sciences, and if the consequences of that worldview are unacceptable, what are the possible alternatives? One alternative would, of course, be to reject science and any possible view of the world which could be founded upon it. Alternatives of this kind have been put forward, in various forms, throughout history. One could embrace different forms of romanticism, intuitionism, mysticism, irrationalism, or fundamentalism. Although alternatives of this kind remain a permanent possibility, it will be the contention of the writer of this paper that another alternative is possible. One could interpret the data of science in a manner entirely different from the manner in which they have been interpreted by the philosophy of positivism. It will be the object of this paper to prove that an entirely different worldview, non-positivistic in scope and very much in accord with true morality, could be erected upon the findings of modern science. As the paper unfolds, it will become clear that many interpreters and analysts of science actually view the experimental, physical sciences through the historical, cultural framework of the nineteenth century and not of the twentieth. Much of what passes today as the worldview of empirical science amounts to a corrupted form of Newtonian mechanics, which is a decadent cultural deposit tracing back to a nineteenth century quasi-scientific view of the world. This view, however popularized, however widely accepted today, is now antiquated. In extremely significant respects it has altogether been replaced by a much broader twentieth century view of science based on twentieth century scientific theories, which originated from foundations entirely or almost entirely non-Newtonian. Concretely, Relativity Theory and Quantum Mechanics, with their combined findings in the physical sciences, were revolutions in the field of science and each of these theories taken singly hold implications for a revolutionary view of what it is that science reports about the nature of reality. This sense of creating a revolution was very much alive when Relativity Theory and Quantum Mechanics came into acceptance, but, at least according to one author, Milie Capek, in his book, The Philosophical Impact of Contemporary Physics, the original sense of creating a revolution in our modes of thinking about the universe has since subsided and we have, in effect, reverted to a more hidebound, Newtonian view of what science is about. It was to rekindle this sense of creating a new revolutionary view of science, that Capek claims he wrote his work in 1961.

The present author is in sympathy with Capek's belief that the idea of a new scientific worldview has retreated from our culture, both in professional philosophy, in popularizations of science, and in our popular culture. The contribution of this paper will lie in its attempt to prove that the new scientific worldview has also never had an adequate chance to enter into our moral interpretation of the universe, because we are still, to a great extent, the unknowing victims of a moral interpretation of the world which is unfortunately narrow—namely, a moral interpretation based upon viewing the world through the eyes of a corrupted Newtonian mechanics. In other words, we still view the world morally, much the same way in which nineteenth century man viewed the world. The ethical impact of twentieth century science has not yet penetrated modern consciousness.

In order to stress just these moral implications of twentieth century science, this paper will first, contrast the special features of the nineteenth and the twentieth century scientific worldviews, respectively. Then, the ethical implications of these features, respectively for nineteenth and twentieth century ethics will be drawn out. Finally, the ultimate impact of twentieth century science upon ethics will be described.

A) Contrast of Two Worldviews

Twentieth century science stands opposed to the science of the nineteenth century in fundamental features. In broad outlines, the science of these different centuries reveals an understanding of the universe which is, in general terms, mutually and diametrically opposed to one another. The reality of the universe, in the perspective of nineteenth century science, is understood in "reductionistic" terms i.e., in terms of its smallest possible elements, its submicroscopic particles, atoms, Atoms in motion, randomly colliding with one another, constitute the explanation of the entire physical universe. These are the fundamental building blocks of matter, and these elementary particles in motion are the foundations of all physical and chemical changes which take place in nature. There are ninety-two natural elements or types of atoms and all chemical compounds are comprised of natural groupings of these. Water, for example, (chemical formula - H_2O), is comprised of two atoms of hydrogen and one atom of oxygen. The solid, liquid, and gaseous state of water can be explained by the rate of motion of the atoms, ice, by slow moving atoms, water, by atoms in more rapid motion, and water vapor, by atoms colliding at high velocities. All physical reality could be reduced to atoms in motion. Sound was simply a compression of atoms in columns of air, and color was simply the impact of energy released from atoms in the form of light waves. In the final analysis, all reality was reduced to particles of matter in motion, existing in space and time. It is an image of the universe which can be easily pictorialized, and , according to Capek, in The Philosophic Impact of Contemporary Physics, it still dominates our imagination today. Our subconscious imagination is, unfortunately, still in proximity to the visual-tactile imagery of commonsence.

However, the reality of the universe is understood from a different perspective in our twentieth century science and this, according to Capek, is not frequently enough understood, either by the layman, by popularizers of science, or by contemporary philosophers of science. The universe, in the perspective of twentieth century science, is a "holistic" universe, in which what is essential to the understanding of nature is not so much the reduction of nature to atoms in motion, existing in space and time, as the interrelationships among the atoms in the perception of the entire field of force in which the atom is located simply as one point of focus in the field. These special implications of twentieth century science are stressed in a publication entitled *Energy Potential: Toward a New Electromagnetic Field Theory* by Carol White. In the "reductionistic" view of the nineteenth century, with its atoms in motion, neat and simple distinctions were stressed, e.g. the neat and simple distinctions between matter and motion, the neat and simple distinctions between space and time. The combined effect of such twentieth century discoveries as Relativity Theory and Quantum Mechanics has been to blur these simple, commonsensical distinctions so that it is no longer possible to picture in imagination small particles in motion surrounded by vast areas of space. The Special Theory of Relativity posited that space and time are interrelated, so that time may be conceived of as a kind of fourth dimension, and the General Theory of Relativity posited that matter and energy seem to be different forms of the same underlying reality, or in Einstein's words, matter is simply put, "relaxed energy". In the "holistic" view, all of the parts are interrelated in the broader field and one particle of matter is related to the fields of energy surrounding it and also to the enveloping space and time of that field. It is not distinct from that field in any simple manner which could be easily pictorialized. Connections and interrelationships, the non-Euclidean geometry of the entire field become vital and our simple commonsensical distinctions pale into insignificance, along with its pictorial imagination. If analogies are needed here, Capek suggests that the auditory imagination might be able to find one in the concept of the melody in which the interconnectedness of the notes into a melodic pattern is plainly what counts and what is, in the long run, pleasing to the ear, much more so than the sound of any of the individual notes, though these may be pleasing also. It is our subconscious imagination, still rooted in the nineteenth century, which still views the universe in terms of atoms in motion and still thinks in terms of individual notes rather than in terms of the entire melody.

Distinguishing features of the nineteenth century "reductionistic" view, which is actually a corruption of Newtonian Mechanics are its atomism, its belief that nature is comprised ultimately of submicroscopic particles, its materialism, its central faith that all reality is ultimately matter, its credo of no action-at-a-distance, the theory that all physical action and reaction must take place by means of proximate, physical contact, its overall sharp distinctions between space, time, matter, and energy, its proximity to the imagery of commonsense both in it sharp distinctions and in its no action-at-a-distance credo, its determinism and mechanicism, here, the creed that nature is no large machine, in which the individual parts of the machine are paramount, and finally, in line with its atomism, an assumption of the casual inertness of matter, i.e., the incapacity of matter to initiate change in an interrelated field rather than being simply the passive receptor of random collisions.

Contemporary or twentieth century science finds an entirely different set of features inherent in the natural universe. Distinguishing features of "holism" are the analysis of "force Fields", the entire surrounding environment of individual phenomena and so-called bits and pieces of matter which becomes all important, a certain, healthy skepticism concerning the ultimate nature of matter since it is so interrelated to space, time, motion, and energy, a credo of action-at-a-distance as set forth by the General Theory of Relativity, basing its imagination here upon field theory rather than upon simple commonsensical experience, a new perception of the interrelatedness of space, time, matter, and motion with its attendant remoteness from the visual imagery of commonsense, its postulation of indeterminacy in regard to the universe, i.e., the universe is no longer viewed as obeying the simple laws of a machine with parts, its organicism, i.e., its sense of the interconnection of all the parts as interrelated, much as the organs in a living being, and finally, because of this sense of interconnectedness, a certain understanding that matter is somehow causally active in relating to the surrounding environment or field.

In twentieth century science, "holism", the sense of the interconnectedness of the universe replaces a "reductionistic", analytical sense of the separateness and distinctness of everything, which latter is an understanding of the universe rooted in our commonsense and in, what may very well amount to the same thing, our natural conservatism. We still hanker back to the perception of the universe and the method of thinking about it prevalent in the nineteenth century, even though our twentieth century science has firmly discredited this scientific worldview.

(B) Impact of Worldviews Upon Ethics

Viewpoints concerning the ultimate structure of the universe rarely remain in the realm of theory. They have practical application. One might contrast the theistic worldview of the Middle Ages with its consequent mysticism and other worldliness with our modern scientific worldview, still a form of Newtonianism, and its consequent technological expertise. Or, it might be possible to view many social reform movements as a consequence of the philosophy of the eighteenth century Enlightenment, or consider, as Max Weber did, the impact of the Protestant theory of predestination upon the rise of capitalism. Many view movements such as socialism and feminism as political offshoots of the Christian worldview.

Paralleling this, it should be a matter of no small surprise that the corpuscular view of matter, that corrupted form of Newtonian mechanics which dominated the nineteenth century, should affect men's ways of thinking and acting. The corpuscular view of matter did, indeed, have such an impact. If the world, if the entire universe, is seen as a mere conglomerate of atoms, human society comes to be looked upon in the same way, as a mere conglomerate of individuals. As the universe is produced by the random collision of atoms, so human society is produced by the random collision of individuals. As the universe follows certain determined chemical and physical laws according to this same random collision of atoms, so human society follows certain highly determined political and economic laws according to the random business transactions of many self-interested individuals, none of whom are particularly related, one to another, by any other tie except market, business-like relationships. Yet the market-place follows well defined economic laws, the laws of supply and demand, the laws of the business cycle with boom and bust. The individuals involved could be likened to social atoms involved in random transactions, who, together create economic laws for a society as well defined, often as susceptible to prediction as the physical laws relating to the volume and heat of gasses, which are, in turn, comprised of physical atoms. The universe, in the reductionistic, atomic worldview is constructed without any overall, organized purpose, without any plan, without any final causality, yet out of this random chaos of particles colliding like billiard balls, or, we might even say, like ping-pong balls emerges all of Isaac Newton's three laws of motion which he posited in the Principia, written in 1684, and which constituted an ultimate explanation of the physical universe for the nineteenth century. In human society, likewise, laissez-faire economics is completely unplanned and, following this theory, human individuals, the social atoms, are allowed maximum freedom in all business transaction. As the physical atom obeys no organized purpose, no final causality, so the human individual, the social atom, obeys no organized moral purpose, no final causality in the area of ethical constraints. The social atom exists without a final moral plan. The moral freedom of the individual obeys no organized plan, and, therefore, it operates without any moral restrictions.

However, in the twentieth century worldview, the organized field has replaced the particle. In order to understand any piece of localized matter, it is necessary to understand, in depth, it's relationship to it's surrounding field. The behavior of the so-called particle is not random in ultimate terms. It's behavior is ultimately related to a physical system of which it is an integral part. Extracted from that system, the physical behavior of the remaining system changes, sometimes radically. The remaining system now has a different space curve, a different gravitational and electromagnetic field. By removing the matter, one changes the surrounding field and hence the entire system with which the matter is integrated as a part of the entire system. Holism and interrelationship among parts replaces reductionism and the individualism of particles. This new scientific worldview could have enormous ramifications in the ethical and social sphere of life, much as the, by now obsolete, Newtonian mechanics, once did, and, unfortunately, still does. It is necessary to abandon obsolete views in the social as well as they physical sphere of reality and to come to the realization that Newtonianism in the social sphere may have served our nineteenth century ancestors well enough but it can no longer serve us. We now perceive the world physically not so much as a collection of particles in motion but as an integrated system. Similarly, it is incumbent upon us to perceive the social world not as a random series of transactions among self interested individuals but as a moral field, a morally interconnected system, based upon a morally organized final purpose—a purpose such as greater communication, greater communion, greater awareness of the moral field of different, unique cultures. It is just this sensitivity to the surrounding social and moral field which Teilhard de Chardin saw as the proper philosophic interpretation of the raw data of biological evolution in his major work, *The Phenomenon of Man*, published in 1958. Why is it necessary to remain rooted in hidebound patterns of moral and social thinking which are based upon an antiquated, nineteenth century view of the world, when in laying this, by now, decadent worldview, to its proper resting place, we could break the bounds of our old provincialism and replace it with moral and social views which are decidedly superior.

A more holistic, ethical view of the world would imply that communalism, a sense of membership in the community of the entire earth would replace older forms of individualism, which are based upon trampling on the legitimate rights of others in order to achieve the next and higher rung in the social ladder. Man, if we were to be truly contemporary and basing ourselves no longer upon an antiquated scientific worldview, but upon a more viable, broader contemporary, would be viewed in terms of his connections, his relationships with citizens of radically diverse cultures on our planet. Objectivistic and altruistic forms of ethics, which recognize the human rights of other people, could replace the current deification in our culture of all forms of human aggression, basing itself upon the human aggressiveness which the decadent, social atom exhibits in the economic marketplace. The simple materialism of the "reductionistic" worldview could be replaced by an intensification of interest in psychic phenomena. For the first time it would be possible to think as contemporary people, as people of the twentieth century, who view the earth in the by-word of the environmental movement as a "spaceship", with limited supplies that must be constantly recycled. The contemporary sense of interconnectedness and system is here emphasized. The "spaceship" image involves intensive planning, i.e., the reallocation of resources from one part of the globe to another. This new holistic contemporary image could make the prevalent commonsensical market calculations of the old Newtonian worldview of simple mechanism, marginal in scope. Man's creativity would be given a grater chance over the simple determinism of the economic market and intense social planning could create final ends for man, and eliminate the mechanistic operations of the "free market". Finally, a hylozoistic sense of the sacredness of nature might replace the corrupt, decadent Newtonian view of nature and matter as causally inert, rather than as vitally related to its immediate field of action.

CONCLUSION: ULTIMATE IMPACT OF 20TH CENTURY SCIENCE UPON ETHICS

In summary, the foregoing reflections amount to what could, if we chose to be contemporary, amount to an eclipse of the analytic, corpuscular view of nature with its attendant individualism and aggressive free market economy, an entire physical and ethical scientific worldview prevalent in the nineteenth century by a synthetic holistic view of nature with its attendant communalism and cooperative, planned economy, more in harmony with a physical and ethical, scientific worldview which springs from our own century. Our natural conservatism may inhibit us. We may very well persist in moribund concepts of what science is all about, and in this endeavor we will no doubt find much in the layman's present conception of science, in contemporary popularizations of science, and also, to a great extent, in the view of science held to by man, contemporary analytic philosophers. But all of these conceptions of what science really is rest upon a narrower, more positivistic, more Newtonian form of it, which is nothing but a cultural accretion from the past. Contemporary science is not inimical to morality and altruism. Newtonian science could often be used as supportive of the laissez-faire, allow the individual to do what he wants including trampling upon the legitimate rights of others, survival of the fittest morality, prevalent today. Contemporary science could be used to support a wider, superior vision of human cooperation, of "Spaceship Earth", of membership in the planet, Earth. Or we may choose ossification in the form of a corrupted Newtonian mechanics of the nineteenth century which could be employed to buttress a "survival of the fittest" mentality. The choice is to remain rooted in decadence or to develop.

CHAPTER TWO

PSYCHIC PHENOMENA AND TWENTIETH CENTURY PHYSICS

Parapsychology has never been considered part of the scientific establishment. Although research conducted in the wide area of psychic phenomena often has yielded well-documented cases of the authenticity of mind-reading incidents, forseeing of future events, spoon-bending at a distance and even the transport of a principal's own body to another distant region, the scientific community almost to a whole remains unconvinced. It is expected and even necessary and required that there should be skepticism since the first obligation scientists hold is to truth. For this reason, scientists insist that all claims made to the authenticity of psychic phenomena events must be fully substantiated by credible evidence that will prove to be test-worthy. Yet, given the very nature of psychic phenomena, can the requirement of verifiable proof be forthcoming of the existence of psychic phenomena such as telepathy, pre-cognition, psychokinesis, levitation and teleportation?

For many years, Duke University has been the center of studies in psychic, or so-called, paranormal phenomena. Many of the obtained results were popularized by J. B. Rhine, Associate Professor of Psychology, in residence in the year 1964 when his book, Extra-Sensory Perception, was published in English. The attendant publicity resulted in widespread interest by the public. However, the large receipts from the sales of the book precipitated the entry into the field of a host of new investigators, culminating in new publications, embracing: clairvoyance, telepathy, precognition, retro-cognition, reincarnation, psychometry, psychokinesis, teleportation and healing. Only recently have serious efforts been made by investigators, including a few of the scientists within the scientific establishment, to separate fact from speculation in the volumes on filed of phenomena events. Results remain inconclusive: consensus being that even though psychic phenomena is not an established actuality, there does remain the possibility for a future acceptance.

The purpose of this writing is neither to attempt to establish the reality of psychic phenomenon, nor to disprove it - either of which would be outside the writer's keen, and in all probability cannot be done at all at this time, but rather to search for and to consider the reasons for the scientific community's continuing proscription on engaging in research in psychic phenomena.

In all areas of life, opinions are determined by assumptions under which individuals conduct themselves from the beginning. For example, almost all decisions reached on issues such as abortion and gun control provide excellent illustrations of the manner in which assumptions govern thinking. Decisions either pro or con, taken in the matter of abortion, are based upon the individual's regard for human life, and the value of that human life with relation to society as a whole.

Acceptance of the fetus as a human being is more or less established. Doctors now working on the saving of the life of the fetus while still in the uterus, refer to "their little patient". For the individual, who stands against abortion, that life in the uterus has value as a human being intrinsically. For the individual, who would opt for abortion, (even though he may consider the unborn as a full human being)- takes into account first the contribution, or the value of that human life to society, i.e., is the baby "unwanted". If so, the baby poses a threat as yet "another mouth to feed", and increases the individual's horror of world overpopulation. In a consideration of "gun control: pro/con, the question is built upon prior assumption under which the individual operates. Those for the right to be armed, and who are against gun control, believe that man is so hopelessly malicious that he will kill anyhow - even without the handy gun. The petitioners for gun control believe man to be a weak creature, prone to hat anger and belabored by unsupportable frustrations and when beset by these propensities are aided and abetted in murder through the environmental factor of a handy gun. A former policeman, turned writer, Wambaugh, in his novel, *The Glitter Dome* states that there are many policemen, who become ghastly suicides by there own handy guns - but that even less than half of the statistics of these worried, harried policemen go on record as suicides.

In similar fashion, the answers given to questions concerning psychic phenomena will be governed by the assumptions originally made. On the basis of certain assumptions, psychic phenomena is a clear impossibility. Whereas, on the basis of assumptions diametrically opposed, psychic phenomena is not only possible, but probable. The original set of assumptions is crucial, and bears on the types of investigations undertaken and the conclusions reached. Since this writing is concerned with the question as to why the scientific establishment was reluctant to concede the possibility of extra-sensory perception (even though a new look by recent research leans to a support of its possibility) perhaps the original assumptions made by the scientific establishment are the key to the answer. Ordinarily, "paranormal phenomena, or extra sensory perception (with emphasis on "extra") suggests a benign magic for others a barbarous, primitive superstition being operative. Yet, to an increasing number, extra sensory perception indicates that man may have experience of a different knowledge outside of the ordinary routes of five senses. In the opinion of many scientists, however, the likelihood of such phenomena would violate a central bastion of Science, namely: "The Verification Principle" of the Vienna Circle of scientist-philosophers. For philosophers, Moritz Schlick, the founder and Carnap and Reichenbach, members of the original Circle, everything not observable by the five senses publicly and as results obtained through tests conducted under scientific laboratory conditions is: Nonsense. Therefore, if mind is considered by researchers in the area of the paranormal as a kind of "sixth" sense, the mind never could be publicly observable under the conditions of the other five senses.

What can be publicly observed, according to a more traditional credo of Science, must be material. Whatever can be observed must occupy space and weight. This is observably true, at least in the sense that nothing can be directly observed without inference unless it is somehow material, occupying space and having weight. On the other hand, it may be possible to infer the existence of what is somehow non-material from what is material. This is the rationale of experiments in psychic phenomena. Nevertheless, there are scientists, who would be extremely cautious in the formulation of like inferences because they operate upon the unclarified or hidden assumptions that whatever exists, that whatever is real must take some form of matter. Since matter is all that can be directly observable, it is the only reality that can be affirmed ultimately to exist. Statements made otherwise would have to be labeled with that favorite pejorative of the Vienna Circle: "Nonsense".

All of the objects with which mankind is familiar are forms of matter, occupying space and having weight and is as true of building trees, etc. as it is of the human body and of the instrument of human thought, the brain. The so-called "mind" is for many scientists and philosophers, such as B. F. Skinner and Wilfred B. Sellars, as well as for the materialistic German philosophers of the nineteenth century, such as Ludwig Buchner, simply an epiphenomenon, or after effect of the brain.

Many scientist of the nineteenth century as well as the twentieth were implicit materialists, holding that the only reality in the universe was comprised of matter in its variegated arrangements. By this is meant that reality consisted entirely of minute, separate, particles too small to be seen with a microscope, called atoms that collide by immediate contact with other atoms. These collisions produced all of the motion and all of the change with which mankind is familiar. "All ordinary objects: buildings, trees, etc.,being comprised of physical minute atoms which are in constant motion and collision with one another" is a description of the natural universe that reveals some of the corollaries of materialism firmly believed in by the scientists of the nineteenth century, and is subscribed to by many scientists today. Holding to these materialistic presuppositions (or assumptions) often without the scientist's full awareness, does not endow that individual with the ability to analyze and subject seemingly outlandish phenomena to a fair and objective consideration. Nor can a completely rational judgment, concerning the validity of paranormal phenomena, be given by a confirmed materialist, who is a person holding to the tacit presupposition, or set presuppositions, that reality is reducible to separate bits and pieces of matter, colliding with one another according to certain determined laws that are predictable. For the individual scientist clinging to like assumptions, out-of-the-body experiences would be deemed impossible since only matter is real. To the materialist, whether or not conscious of his assumptions, the ability to manipulate objects from a distance would be unacceptable since one of the corollaries of materialism describes reality as group of atoms that must be in physical contact with other atoms in order to move them. In this manner, the physical atoms, comprising the human hand, must be direct, physical contact with the atoms of the spoon in order to cause the spoon to be moved. If the assumptions of materialism with reference to the nature of the universe are correct, then paranormal phenomena do constitute an impossibility. If everything is comprised of minute particles in motion, then teleportation, psychokinesis and clairvoyance are absurdities.

Now, as to why so very many scientists have claimed that the description of the real is exhausted by matter-in-motion, and to focus on the answer. Consider today's scientific establishment that is heir to the assumptions of nineteenth century physics, operating almost entirely upon materialistic premises that rationally explained the physical universe. In the twentieth century, the materialistic assumptions of science are workable in providing explanations of a limited range of phenomena. Therefore, it is understandable that many scientists continue to believe in assumptions that proved to be successful in the past and even into the present. Why should they not remain a model for future research since the materialistic model has proven its worth, it may be the correct description of the universe, and certainly should not be discarded until totally disproven?

The materialistic world view, or picture of the universe, has indeed proven its mettle within ordained areas of human experience. For example, the physics of the nineteenth century can be employed mathematically to predict the orbits of moon and planets with reasonable accuracy, but today astronomers are interested more in learning about the behavior and activity of more distant stellar objects, such as the mysterious quasars, objects of unknown origin, the light from which may take as long as ten billion years to reach this planet. For such purposes, nineteenth century physics is outmoded. In its stead scientists will employ the fourth dimensional geometry of Einstein's Relativity Theory. Relativity Theory is, to a great extent, a product of the science of the twentieth century, even though the mathematical foundations of the theory were laid in the nineteenth century with the discovery of fourth and fifth dimensional geometry by Riemann and Lobachevsky, Einstein did not publish the results of the Special Theory of Relativity until 1905, and the results of the General Theory appeared for the first time in 1915. To astronomers engaged in work on distant interstellar objects, the physics of the nineteenth century would prove moribund for their purposes.

The physics involved in Relativity Theory is of interest not only for its own sake, but also for the assumptions on which it rests that are not at all the commonsensical assumptions of nineteenth century science. For the physics of the twentieth century, it is possible for objects to influence one another physically without physical contiguity, and in scientific circles is known as "action-at-a-distance". For twentieth century science "action-at-a-distance" has become an accepted assumption. Additionally, there is another perspective in relationship to ordinary objects inherent in Relativity Theory. Relativity Theory effectively represents the demoliton of a favorite assumption present in all of nineteenth century science, labeled by the great philosopher, Whitehead, as "the fallacy of simple location." This "fallacy" amounts to the commonsensical belief that any physical object-buildings, trees, etc. - can be in one place only at any given time. Contemporary scientists have learned (through the discovery of Einstein's Relativity) that space is related to time, and that matter is related to motion. These four elements of the natural, physical universe are not distinct, separate entities - but, are interrelated and interconnected to one another. The conclusion drawn by man commentators on Relativity is a new perception of the significance of the electromagnetic and gravitational field surrounding the individual atom. For twentieth century physics, the concept of "field" is paramount. The "field" surrounding the given individual minute particle, the atom, is ultimately central to the understanding of the physical universe, and the concept of the atom, the individual particle becomes secondary. The universe of twentieth century physics is no longer the universe of minute particles or atoms in motion. The material, physical atom is an integral part of the surrounding field. It is no longer the hard, material particle of nineteenth century physics - now, there is a sense in which it may be said to be the surrounding field. The nineteenth century concept of the simple particle which was in one definite place at one definite time has been replaced by the concept of the surrounding "field", or general region, of which "field", or region, the atom is an integral part. The overriding importance of the concept of "field" in the science of the twentieth century was that its acceptance dealt the blow that completely destroyed one of the most cherished and accepted beliefs with reference to the physical universe of the nineteenth century, namely: "the fallacy of simple location". One object, can, in a certain sense, be in more than one place at any one given time, meaning that the building is definitely what it is, a building, but there is also a sense in which it is the tree, etc. since there is a sense in which the building is also a part of the surrounding "field". Therefore, the "fallacy of simple location" is a nineteenth century fallacy - commonsensical though the concept may be.)

The demolition of "no -action-at-a-distance" and acceptance of the fallacy of "simple location", represent radical replacements of at least two nineteenth century assumptions: the assumption of "no-action-at-a-distance" and the assumption of "simple location". When these assumptions fell into disrepute so did nineteenth century physics.

Returning to the matter of psychic phenomena, such as clairvoyance, psychokinesis and teleportation, the very possibility of these is based upon the twin premises of action-at-a-distance and the fallacy of simple location, the relationship of the object to its surrounding field. Destroy these premises and psychic phenomena itself becomes a fallacy. With acceptance, there is nothing absurd, outlandish or irrational about granting credence to at least the plausibility of psychic occurrences in which the objects or the persons involved do not enter into physical contact with one another and in which the individual body of the human person is in more than one place at any one, definite time.

Working under the assumptions of the science of the nineteenth century, it is irrational to grant to any aspect of paranormal phenomena sympathetic hearing; whereas, operating under the assumptions of twentieth century physics nothing could be more rational than adoption of an open-minded, flexible and receptive mentality in the pursuit of these investigations. Inherent natural conservatism locks persons within the confines of certain nineteenth century commonsensical assumptions governing the world; consequently, closes minds to the very possibility of clairvoyance, psychokinesis and teleportation. However, the broader and deeper knowledge of the physical universe accruing as a result of the developments should eventually attune man's mind to the internally coherent logic underlying the study of any area of psychic phenomena. Accepting the assumptions of twentieth century science clairvoyance, psychokinesis, teleportation and similar manifestations make sound sense, although stating this is not to accept the reality of these events without question.

****

The mechanistic model of the universe, held by many in the nineteenth century, began to change gradually so that today many scientists no longer subscribe to the mechanistic model. It is an integral principle of the mechanistic model that space, time, motion and matter must be conceived of as separate parts as of a machine. However, the physics of the twentieth century strongly anticipates that they are not separate, but to the contrary, are interrelated phases of the same system. The basic springboard for the emergence of this more sophisticated consciousness of the universe was probably the discovery of hitherto unknown forms of geometry: the geometry of the fourth and fifth dimensions by two mathematicians of the nineteenth century: Riemann and Lobachevsky. The geometry of Euclid can be imagined on a sense basis, but the ordinary consciousness balks at a geometry seeming to go beyond even the limits of human imagination. However, men of a mathematical bent foresaw some of the new worlds that were being disclosed by the possibilities presented. Mathematicians found no reason, mathematically, why a universe of three dimensions should exist and that no further dimensions be considered. Many writers toward the close of the nineteenth and the beginning of the twentieth century, such as C. H. Hinton[1], P.D. Ouspensky[2] speculated that the universe could actually be a four dimensional one, and that if man sharply coned his intellectual powers, he might be able to perceive things in this new way. Employing the title of C. H..Hinton's book, published in 1888, there was emerging on the horizon, *A New Era of Thought*.

The downfall of the mechanistic, atomic theory of the universe probably began with the Michelson-Morley experiment of the 1880's and 1890's. Michelson and

Morley were two scientist, who wanted to test the effects of the so-called "ether drag" on the speed of light. It was known that sound travelled through a medium, the surrounding air, and that its speed could be slowed through the velocity and or "drag" of the wind. At that time, it was not known what the medium was in which light travelled, but if the mechanistic view of the universe governed, light waves that travelled from a light source had to set up the wave-like vibrations in something. This "something" was called "ether", although never detected through any scientific experiment. Therefore, Michelson and Morley attempted such an experiment. They tried to detect the "ether" by measuring the force of its drag on the speed of light. Light travelled much faster than sound, 186,000 miles per second, roughly compared to the speed of sound, 1,100 feet per second, roughly. For the experiment to work, a complex set of rotating mirrors had to be set up, miles apart, and two light sources deflected in different directions. The experimenters reasoned that at least one of the beams (because of the different directions) had to encounter the so-called "ether drag", and the relative discrepancy in the velocity of the two beams could then be compared. To the chagrin of the scientific community discrepancy was not detected, nor was there an "ether drag". Were the detection devices not sophisticated enough? Did one or both experimenters make mistakes?[3]

One theory, named the Lorentz-Fitzgerald Contraction Theory after the scientists who postulated it, represented a last ditch effort to preserve the mechanistic model of the universe. The major claim was that an "ether drift" was not detected because objects contract, actually become smaller, in the direction of their motion.[4] This was correct, but the explanation given for the shrinkage was still in terms of the mechanistic image of the "ether drift".

Einstein's Special Theory of Relativity destroyed the mechanistic concept of the ether, and subsequently, the entire mechanical model of the nineteenth century established universe. In seeming defiance of all commonsensical mechanistic images of physical reality, Einstein claimed that motion was not absolute in the sense in which scientists, following in the footsteps of Newton, had thought of motion, but was relative to the observer. Hence, the speed of light was always roughly 186,000 miles per second, relative to the observer, no matter what his speed, or direction of motion. Motion, he stressed, in the Theory of Special Relativity, was relative, and so was space and matter and time.[5] Space, matter and time were not distinct entities, but all three were related to and relative to motion. For this reason, objects approaching the speed of light would experience the "Time Dilation Effect", the actual retardation or slowing down of time. An individual travelling in a spaceship at roughly 170,000 m.p.s. (9/10ths the speed of light) for a period of ten years (his time) could return to earth, conceivably, only to learn that his friends, etc. have aged by twenty years.

Now...commonsense mechanism has been replaced by the twentieth century physics of interrelated elements upon which the General Theory of Relativity expanded[6]. Toward the end of his life, Einstein was busy formulating his General Field Theory, his attempt to relate light, gravity and electromagnetism into the one all encompassing general "field" of which the universe is comprised, and is not a machine, but an interrelated system[7]. The universe of Relativity is the universe of the macrocosm, the universe if massive, and far distant stellar object, but even on the level of the microsm, the infinitesimal world of atomic and subatomic particles the mechanistic image was dealt a death blow.

In 1931, the scientist Werner Heisenberg, put forth his Uncertainty Principle as explanation for the experimenter's almost insuperable difficulty in predicting both the position and the motion of an electron, the subatomic particle orbiting around the atom. Since no experimenter was able to predict both position and velocity with equal precision, Heisnberg presented his theory in explanation. Prediction was deemed impossible because subatomic particles do not always behave with law-like regularity. There is about them an uncertainty, which is part of the structure of nature itself, and the uncertainty in prediction has nothing to do with limitations in either the observer or in his equipment. Only if the physical world is conceived of as a machine, running like clockwork, is nature and every other being within it thought of as following determined laws, enabling man to predict the behavior of the object. In the opinion of philosopher Milic Capek, the position and motion of the particle cannot be predicted because there is no particle, or segment of mater that is completely distinct from space and motion and time. Man would do better to be rid of atomic theory and conceive of nature in terms of surrounding "fields", the four dimensional space-time matrix, with which the so-called particle is interconnected and interrelated.

Today, the universe of contemporary physics is not viewed as a large machine, but more like an organism in which the parts are vital to the whole and vice versa. To repeat: space, time, matter and motion are not discrete, separate elements of the universe. Space, time and matter depend upon motion. All four are interrelated in a manner not too unlike the manner in which the organs of the body are related to the whole[8].

The image of the world of the nineteenth century, at least of the scientific world, is not all the image of the world that has been presented for that of the twentieth century. Quasi-philosophical world view, culled from the data of the sciences in any given era often have an impact on many disciplines outside of the sciences, i.e., on the arts, economics, etc. This is true of the contrasting philosophical views built on the respective scientific foundations of the nineteenth and twentieth centuries. The respective image of the nineteenth century of universe as machine and that of the twentieth century as organism stand diametrically opposed.

As stated, the science of the nineteenth century was materialistic. The universe was conceived of as a machine, comprised of material parts, and the material parts of the universe were atoms which were in constant motion within the surrounding space and existed in time. Almost the whole of the familiar change and motion within the universe was the natural consequence of small atoms randomly colliding into one another. For change to take place (outside of the influence of gravitation for which a mechanistic explanation was attempted), the atoms, like ping-pong balls had to make physical contact with one another. Also, the atom could be in only one place at any one time. In other words, the atom in motion was a particle, discrete and separate and entirely distinct from the surrounding space, from its motion, and from the time in which it existed.

In many ways, the physics of the twentieth century is in complete opposition and stands in bold relief against these assumptions. Today, there is a pervading skepticism among scientists concerning the validity of materialism. Also, physicists are not quite so certain what matter is; many consider matter simply as a curve in the surrounding field of space-time.[10] The "field", the interrelated system is much more important than matter to most contemporary scientists because the "Uncertainty Principle" has to a great degree replaced the more traditional, nineteenth century image of a completely determined universe, operating on every level, according to well-defined laws. Physical laws are understood by many of those operating in the realms of microcosm, of quantum mechanics, as nothing more than averages of the indeterminate motions of many sub-atomic particles. No longer is the universe conceived as being the mere conglomerate motions of billions of discrete, separate particles known as atoms, but as an interconnected, four dimensional space-time matrix, in which matter, space, time and motion are all interrelated.[11]

In order for change to occur, atoms no longer must be in physical contact with one another.[12] Change takes place in the interconnected system that the universe is; the change taking place in field, the concept of which occupies much more attention in the thought of atomic physicists today than does the concept of the particle. Because of this, physical contact is not necessary either for change to take place - or, for motion to occur. "Action-at-a-distance" is possible because of the existence of the "field". The existence of the "field" makes it possible also for any given atom, particle, or, any given object, to be in more than one place at one given time.

To compare the foundations of the nineteenth century science with those of the twentieth century, please not the contrasts. Nineteenth century science was based upon the pillars of materialism, determinism, atomism, "no-action-at-a-distance and Whitehead's "Fallacy of Simple Location". Twentieth century science repudiates every one of these pillars of nineteenth century wisdom. Twentieth century science's pillars are constituted by a certain skepticism concerning materialism, indeterminism, a philosophy of the interconnectedness of the interconnectedness of the physical universe in which the parts resemlbe the organs of an organism in the interconnectedness, action-at-a-distance and the field theory.[13]

THE PHILOSOPHICAL FOUNDATIONS
OF PARANORMAL PHENOMENA

Foundations make a difference in man's thinking. What is thought concerning the foundations of nineteenth and twentieth century science, respectively, strongly conditions what is held to be valid, credible and viable regarding psychic phenomena. Again, there is no wish to establish any dogmatic claims for truth, the purpose is to establish the rather strong viability of psychic phenomenon and its seeming credibility. Therefore, it is the time for describing many of the better know types of paranormal phenomena and to compare these types. Yet, if after the types are described, and it seems evident that these seemingly strange events of psychic phenomena lack creditability, it is cautioned that the reaction may be because of an innate conservatism of patters of thought in which the science of the nineteenth century is clung to and which is dubbed with the appellation "common sense", even though that century's science was based upon a less adequate knowledge of the iniverse, and has since proven itself antiquated in many areas of research. The nineteenth century scientific world view is no longer viable and credible as a research model with which to explore psychic phenomena, but the foundations of twentieth century science to constitute this requirement. Types of psychic phenomena are: Clairvoyance, pre-cognition and retro-cognition which can be considered together because of their family resemblances. All three. All three relate to different portions of time, and all three relate to forms of knowledge that are not acquired through the mind alone. Clairvoyance is a type of extra-sensory perception that relates to the present. Here, the subject has knowledge of the characteristics of a physically distant object in the present, which knowledge could not have been obtained through the ordinary channels of the five senses.[14] Telepathy is often classified as a subdivision of clairvoyance, especially a form of communication through mind reading between two or more subjects, both temporarily located in the present, but separated physically by distance.[15] Pre-cognition is a form of prophecy, which relates to the future. It consists of the ability to foretell future events, not, however, through the ordinary rational means of the shrewd or the educated guess.[16] Retro-cognition deals with the past, being the ability to identify with past events in history, or with a particular individual who existed in the past. Such identification does not necessarily imply that the subject, who has the intuition of persons who existed long ago, was that person in reality.[17] Reincarnation, however, which is often classified as a sub-type of retro-cognition, does imply this form of identity with a personage who really existed in the past.[18] Psychometry, another interesting variation, consists of the ability to decipher the past history of an object without any previous knowledge or acquaintance with its history.[19]

To round out this informal description: healing, psychokinesis and teleportation are all concerned with the manipulation and change of inanimate objects and of the human body. There are many documented cases in this century of persons who have possessed healing powers, and who have effected seemingly miraculous cures of diseases in the bodies of others, apparently without response to any of the ordinary means of medical science. Psychokinesis may prove even more interesting in reference to the purposes of this writing, which involves the abililty to manipulate objects in the distance.[20] A classic experimental trick here involves the bending of spoons from a physical distance, without employment of the usual motor or sensory means. Teleportation, the ability to physically transport oneself to different places - perhaps to different times - while also remaining in one's present location, which is perhaps the most intriguing of these possibilites. An account of these experiences, entitled *Journeys Out of the Body*, was published in 1973 by Robert A. Monroe.[21] It is well worthwhile reading, withholding full credence withal!

This concludes the informal typology of psychic phenomena, and the writer returns to the purposes stated, and will single out Psychokinesis and teleportation to examine in the light of the science of the nineteenth and of the twentieth centuries. Psychokinesis and teleportation, as simply two of the more intriguing types of paranormal phenomena, are both plainly in conflict with most, if not all of the assumptions of nineteenth century science. In both cases, either inanimate objects, or the human body itself, is being changed or moved in non-materialistic ways, i.e., without the direct intervention of matter in the form of a material object. Focusing upon psychokinesis, here material objects are being changed, manipulated and physically moved from a distance. Taking up once again the area of teleportation: Herein, the human body simultaneously co-exists in two, or possibly more, places at once. All of these reputed occurrences are unacceptable - within the context of nineteenth century science. Psychokinesis and teleportation violate many of the assumptions of nineteenth century science, including its materialism, its dictum of no action-at-a-distance, and its blind acceptance of what Whitehead labelled, "the fallacy of simple location".[22]

If placed within the context of the more advanced science of the twentieth century, the seemingly fantastic phenomena of psychokinesis and even more especially the phenomena of teleportation, become feasible, viable, credible possibilities in the context of the universe which is understood much better today. Twentieth century science exhibits skepticism concerning materialism; it accepts "action-at-a-distance", and, in general, does not make that blunder (even though commonsensical) which the philosopher Whitehead labelled as "the fallacy of simple location". Proof of this is the manner in which today's science boldly accepts "field" theory. Therefore, both psychokinesis and teleportation, as two of the more pronounced kinds of paranormal phenomena, can coherently fit into the assumptions of twentieth century science. Neither one of which operates within the boundaries of materialism, and both involve forms of change that do not seem to be influenced by matter. Psychokinesis involves action-at-a-distance, that cardinal violation of nineteenth century science. Teleportation, the abililty of the human body to be in more than one place at any one time, plainly violates "simple location". Phenomenon, such as teleportation, could fit coherently and rationally into a form of "field" theory, that is central to the science of the twentieth century, and, again, is an expression of the abandonment of yet another form of nineteenth century erroneousness, "the Fallacy of Simple Location".

Man's instincts are, more often than not, conservative. This is why psychic or paranormal phenomena is found to be perplexing, jarring man's commonsense understanding of the physical universe. This commonsense, as has been stated, is more likely than not a remnant of nineteenth century assumptions about science that has become rooted in the conservative part of man's subconscious imagination. Spontaneously and instinctively, time, space, matter and motion are thought of as separate entities. "Action-at-a-distance" is thought impossible. All change and movement of any kind are considered resulting from a form of physical contact, including the moon's gravitational influence on the tides. Any violation of "simple location" is deemed a desertion of man's reasoning powers.

NEVERTHELESS, the physics of the twentieth century has taught mankind. Some day it may be successful in teaching that the entire range of psychic phenomena, including psychokinesis and teleportation, almost incredible though it may seem, somehow fit the mold of twentieth century science. Presuppositions of nineteenth century science that had become glued to instinctive conservatism will have to be abandoned. Then mankind can well ponder how strange occurrences such as psychic phenomena, actually mesh with a coherent and rational view of the universe, revealed by the experience of the last seventy-five years through the realm of contemporary physics.

PART TWO

PROBLEMS

CHAPTER THREE

THE MIND: IS IT MERELY THE ACTIVITY OF THE BRAIN?

In much of contemporary scientific thought, the ''mind', as an entity separate from the activity and workings of the brain does not exist except as the product of long dated mythologies which ultimately stem from one or another of the world religions. The 'mind' in this tradition of scientific thinking, should be considered as simply the shorthand language which we employ to refer to the activities of the brain. The mind is the equivalent of and is entirely reduceable to the activity of the brain. To think of it otherwise is to be subject to one form of heresy in scientific circles.

According to one tradition of scientific thought, embodied so well in Gilbert Ryle's Concept of Mind, to consider the 'mind' as somehow elevated above, distinct from the activities of the brain is to be guilty of heresy of the 'ghost in the machine', a form of pre-scientific thinking. The often repeated fallacy of the 'ghost in the machine', in plain terms amounts to that perception of the human person, which our commonsense modes of thought often endorse, as, in reality, somehow two things, a 'mind' and a 'body'. The 'mind', according to this tradition, is a separate entity, which directs the activity of the 'body'. The 'mind' gives the commands: the 'body' obeys. If one adheres to this view of the human person, its detractors will often claim that the mind seems to serve the function of a 'ghost' directing the activities of a lifeless body, which can now be compared to a 'machine'. It has long been scientific dogma for many that there is no 'ghost' in the machine. To the contrary, all the machinery of the body can adequately function on its own as an autonomous entity, without any need for intervening 'ghost', to direct its activities, so to speak, from the outside. The machinery of the 'body' is a self-governing, autonomous unit.

The mythology of the ''ghost in the machine' was replaced by another mythology, the mythology which still prevails in scientific circles, but which has recently encountered some questioning and criticism. This is the tradition of reductionism, the attempt to reduce the reality of the mind and all language associated with the mind to the activity of all the nerve is located in the brain and central nervous system.

Ryle exemplifies reductionism perfectly in his *Concept of Mind* through the employment of the example of Oxford University. He asks his readers to imagine a tour through all of the buildings of Oxford by an imaginary guide. After the visitor has seen each of the buildings, he then mentions that he has seen Christ's College, etc., but now he would like to see Oxford University because he still has not seen it. So far, he has merely seen all of the individual buildings. Now, from Ryle's point of view and from the point of view of the rest of us (or so it seems), what the visitor is asking is pure nonsense. He has already seen Oxford University, for the University is merely the sum of all the buildings which comprise it. What our visitor has committed, according to Ryle, is a "category mistake". He has assumed that Oxford University is a thing or an entity over and above and also separate from the buildings which comprise it.

The same kind of category mistake can be made, according to Ryle, in reference to discourse concerning the mind. It is possible to think of the mind as an entity over and above the visible, physical, and separate manifestations of it in behavior. However, the mind, in Ryle's opinion, is nothing but the sum of all its particular behavioral manifestations throughout a given period. It is not some invisible ghost outside the machine, directing all of its activities as a separate substance. The mind is reduceable to all of the separate acts of it behavior. The mind is its publicly manifest, publicly observable behavior and nothing more.

Ryle is a representative of the reductionist doctrine of the mind par excellence. For the reductionist, the mind is the sum of its physical manifestations and nothing more. The doctrine of reductionism has become scientific orthodoxy in certain circles. It has been more recently expressed in Karl Sagan's *The Dragons of Eden,* in which Sagan expresses the viewpoint that we cannot think of the mind as anything more than the neurophysiological activity of the brain.

The doctrine of reductionism has always found its opposition in so-called 'ghost in the machine' theories of the mind. Theories that the mind as a separate entity directs the activity of the body are known as mind-body dualism, or more simply, dualism. Even today, the theory of dualism find adherents. The philosopher, Karl Popper and the brain surgeon, John Eccles have recently collaborated in a book entitled *The Self and Its Brain* (New York: Springer Verlag, 1977). In this work, the surgeon John Eccles, claims that in thirty years of work on the neurophysiology of the brain, he has been unable to account for the existence of man's higher functions in terms of the brain. The brain, for him, is not the equivalent of the mind but a substance independent of the brain. Also, in an article in the August, 1980 issue of Psychology Today, entitled "Rediscovering the Mind", author Harold J. Morowitz defend the view that contemporary physics has reinserted the role of the observer in interpreting the events of the natural universe. Physical events appear to be mind-dependent. This seems to contradict the tendency of many biologists today to reduce the activity of the mind to the physiology of brain cells. For biologists, mind appears to be dependent on matter, but for physicists, matter once again appears to be dependent upon mind. For Morowitz, this is the way scientists have come full circle within the last century to the rediscovery of the mind. It may not, in the long run, be simply a form of matter.

For all of these reasons, recent research into the physiology of the brain and on the frontiers of physics, have tended to place well established doctrine of reductionism in doubt. Is the mind merely the activity of the brain? The contemporary debate takes place in the context of reductionists who claim that it is and of certain modern dualists who claim that, to the contrary, the mind is a separate substance.

It is possible to adapt an intermediary position, that is, to claim that although the mind may not be reduceable to anything that we could call atoms and molecules, it is nevertheless not a ghost which can exist independently of the brain. In their publication, *The Mind's Eye: Fantasies and Reflections on Self and Soul,* authors Douglas R. Hofstadter and Daniel C. Dennett, have compiled a series of contemporary writings which treat of the problem of personal identity. Through the employment of personal commentaries in their role as editors, the thesis that the mind may be compared to a form of "software", very much like the "software" of a computer program, is elaborated with some persuasive arguments. As the program of a computer is not reduceable to the electronic circuitry of which the computer is composed, so the mind is not reduceable to the atoms and molecules of the brain. But similarly, as the program if not entity existing independently of the computer, neither is the mind an entity separate from the brain.

It is this writer's intention to cast some doubt on the thesis of Hofstadter and Dennett, although their thesis is admittedly some improvement over Reductionism. Is not the so-called "software" of the computer somehow independent of the small metal box with all its electronic gadgetry? Since it can exist independently of the "hardware" of that computer, i.e., of the small metal box itself, why not consider the "software" as an independent substance, in the same manner in which the mind may be considered to be an independent substance in philosophical dualism? The purpose of this article will be to question the still reigning orthodoxy of reductionism as well as many of those intermediary positions such as those proposed by Hofstadter and Dennett. In seeing the weaknesses of intermediary positions such as these, it may be possible to propose once again what has for a long time been an ancient philosophical tradition dating back to Plato, the tradition of philosophic dualism. Are there any reasons in this world dominated by contemporary science to believe that dualism, an ancient doctrine emanating from the time of Plato, is a workable version of the world and of man? By tracing the tradition of the soul in Plato, Plotinus and the neo-Platonic school in outline form, then contrasting this tradition with more modern forms of holism and reductionism, I hope to point to some of the flaws in the often placidly accepted reductionist doctrine. Next, it will be necessary to consider the alternative proposed by Hofstadter and Dennett, the theory of the mind as "software" program directing the "hardware" of the body. I propose to show just where this theory is defective, namely in explaining how any "program" is completely dependent for its existence upon that which it programs, and to substitute an alternative, old-fashioned dualism in a new guise. The form of dualism which I will propose can, I believe, effectively deal with one problem that the theory of the mind as program, (the theory of Hofstadter and Dennett), finds intractable, namely the problem of individuality. We will begin with the theory of the soul as it existed in the ancient philosophical world, the doctrine of Plato and Plotinus.

The Tradition of the Soul in Plato and Plotinus

As Hofstadter and Dennett themselves take care to point out, the concept of the soul is considered today to be pre-scientific, although it found its flowering for hundreds of years in philosophical speculations of the ancient Greek world. The origin of the conception of the soul probably originated in Plato, who lived in the fourth century, B.C. It is at least in Plato that we find the first clear conceptual expression of this notion. Plato was a firm dualist, holding to perhaps the most extreme form of this doctrine which can be found in the philosophical literature.

Plato, like his philosophical mentor, Socrates, considered the body as the prison-house of the soul. The goal of the philosopher was to release himself from this prison, a goal adequately achieved only in death. The true philosopher, according to Plato, longed for death, because this was the true release of the soul from the body. In the speculation of Plato, the body presented to man the material world, the world of the five senses, the world of sight, hearing, taste, touch, and smell. This world, the material world of the body, was not the real world because it was a constantly changing world. It did not resemble the world which was known to the mind or the intellect alone, the World of Ideas. When the mind conceived of truth, Justice, or Beauty, it conceived of an Unchanging World which was not restricted to the concrete and the particulars of sight, hearing, smell, touch and taste. The World of Ideas was alone the real world, and it was this world that the Mind or Intellect alone comprehended.

Upon the death of the body, the mind was either released into the World of Ideas or it became reincarnated into another body. When the mind or the Intellect learned such concepts as Truth, Beauty, Justice, Equality, or Goodness, it was simply recollecting or remembering its previous existence in the World of Ideas. The World of Ideas was imperishable, not subject to change, and likewise the Intellect which perceived this world imperishable, not subject to change.

But Plato's most celebrated argument for the immortality of the Soul is set forth in his dialogue, the Meno. It is in the Meno, through the mouth of his mentor, Socrates, that Plato compares the soul to the harmony of the body, like the notes of a melody plucked on a lyre. The soul cannot be destroyed at the moment of death any more than it is possible to destroy the harmony of which a melody consists by physical means. However, it is Meno himself who raises the objection that it may nevertheless be possible to claim that the harmony of the body may no longer be capable of existing after the body's dissolution and decay any more than the melody of the lyre can exist if all the strings of the lyre are broken.

In so many ways, Meno appears to have been the first of the Reductionists. The basic form of his argument has been repeated throughout the centuries by countless materialists who seek to equate the mind with the activity of the underlying lyre, the brain. Some variant of the same doctrine is even presented in The Mind's Eye of Hofstadter and Dennett. Even though neither of these would dream of reducing the mind's activity to that of the brain, they nevertheless do equate mind with the "program" or the harmony of the body.

Is Meno's argument convincing? Is it true that this "harmony of the body" is as dependent upon it as is the melody upon the lyre? The reply to Meno's objection put into the mouth of Socrates has supplied fuel for controversy ever since. According to Socrates, the soul is not merely an entity which is acted upon, as the melody is acted upon by the harp strings. On the contrary, the soul moves the body and directs all of its activities. It is not the passive element in the human person; it is the active element. The soul is not the result of the harmony of the body; it is the cause of the body's harmony. As such, it is not dependent upon the body, and cannot be said to decay with the body. It is precisely this element of the soul's self-activity which materialists and reductionists of all varieties have sought to dispute. The mind or soul, for them, is not self active at all. It is rather the epiphenomenon, or the effect of the body's activity. Where this position is essentially defective is a point with which I would like to take issue at a later point in this essay.

The Philosopher, Plotinus, who lived in the third century, A.D., considered that he did nothing more than to record the true meaning of the doctrine of Plato. Many late commentators have not believed Plotinus but be this as it may, it was Plotinus who provided some of the best arguments in this tradition of philosophical dualism for the independent existence of the soul and for its consequent immortality. In his collected works, which are known as the Enneads, convincing reasons are provided for believing in the soul's immateriality. Everything material is comprised of parts, but can we confidently assert that this is true of the soul? Is it comprised of parts, like every material object with which we are familiar? In the opinion of Plotinus, the soul is aware of every part of itself. When the foot ails, the entire soul is aware of it for the hand moves to soothe it, the eye is aware of the hand and directs it toward the foot. Our contemporary explanation of this phenomena might be simply in terms of the physiology of the brain and central nervous system. Messages are sent by the nerves in the foot to the centralized part of the nervous system, the brain, which effectively regulates all further muscular motion in the direction of the foot. But the remaining difficulty seems to consist of the question as to why we perceive the pain in the foot and not in the brain? Can our contemporary knowledge of physiology really explain this? It appears to this author that it cannot.

The tradition inaugurated by Plato, became in the writings of Plotinus and others a long, distinguished influence upon early Christianity. Through the writings of the early Fathers of the Church, it became the dominant influence in the Christian West for a period of about a thousand years. The Platonic World of Ideas was considered to be an emenation of the mind of God by Augustin, Bishop of Hippo, and the immortality of the soul became a part of Church Doctrine. The Church mystical tradition which considered the finite, visible world as man's illusory, temporal home was an expression of new-Platonism. The realm of eternal values was placed in the transtemporal world, the World of Ideas.

The long, vast neo-Platonic tradition counts among its most outstanding representatives such philosophers as Anselm and Dun Scotus Erigena, to mention only those most well known. In the early twentieth century, the scholar Dean Inge held that the Church had definitely lost something of values when this tradition receded into the background after the early Middle Ages. However, from this venerable tradition, the theory of the existence and the immortality of the soul became widespread and is held by many even today.

The Contemporary Phase: Holism vs. Reductionism

In the contemporary world, behaviorist psychology, dominated by B. F. Skinner, probably represents the reductionist philosophy better than any other individual. Gilbert Ryle and Karl Sagan may be considered s other representatives of the same tradition. For Skinner, the mind is a fiction, a remnant of pre-scientific modes of thinking. The Hellenic tradition of the soul, which Skinner correctly attributes to the speculation of the ancient Greek philosophers, consisted of a dualism, a 'ghost in the machine', which was not supported by empirical research.

The mind, for Skinner, was simply a bundle of S-R Patterns. When you place your hand on a hot stove and instinctively draw it away, this is an example of stimulus-response. The stimulus consists of the hot stove; your response was the act of jerking away your hand. In neurophysiological terms, the brain is supposed to work in the same way. The stimulus is any sensation from the external world, any sensation of heat or cold, of color, or of sounds, which travel along the nerves of the central nervous system, setting off the motor response of the central storage bundle of nerves and fibers, the brain itself. The motor response of the brain consists in sending a message to the nerves of the arm, triggering the arm to jerk away from the stove. This is a classic example of stimulus-response from a behavioral psychologist. Other examples would include such automatic response patterns as the knee-jerk reflex, the blocking reflex, sneezing, etc. In each of these cases, a neural stimulus triggers off a given response.

In the case of the knee-jerk reflex, the stimulus on the nerve endings of the skin, triggered off by a small hammer automatically sets off the motor response in the muscles to jerk the knee, and this response emanates from the central nervous system. Concerning the so called blocking reflex, the stimulus of an oncoming moving vehicle such as a bus or a car triggers off the automatic motor response of blocking car or bus by guarding the body with the arms. Considering the act of sneezing, a certain irritant as stimulus triggers the nervous response of the sneeze.

But what is the connection between stimulus-response and the mind? The mind, for Skinner as well as for any behavior psychologist is nothing but millions of stored stimulus-response patterns. Stimuli from the past along with their potential responses are stored in the nervous system, until they are triggered by appropriate stimuli to make an external motor response. One stores the stimuli in the newspaper advertising a certain movie, and these stimuli in the course of time will trigger the motor response of attending the movie.

Very much as for Gilbert Ryle, for Skinner the mind is simply the sum of all its behavioral manifestations. The mind, apart from the activity of the brain, central nervous system and body, is a fiction. The most representative form of reductionism in the contemporary world will consist of the claim made by behavioral psychologist that the mind is nothing more than the sum of all of its stimulus-response mechanisms or patterns of behavior.

Behaviorist psychology has been vigorously opposed by a small group of psychologists and psychiatrists who are collectively labelled as the humanistic psychologists. Included in this group are such names as Abraham Maslow, Karl Rogers, and Rollo May. All of these claim that human behavior cannot be completely understood in terms of its smaller psychological units, such as the elementary and simple stimulus-response pattern. It is necessary to attempt to understand the human personality as a whole, as an entirety. We cannot accomplish this task if we constantly seek to analyze the human personality in terms of its smallest possible psychological units, stimulus response patterns. For when we attempt to explain human behavior in terms of these very small units, it is difficult to understand how all of these psychologically minute patterns become co-ordinated toward the accomplishment of any unified purpose.

At the same time, it appears obvious that human motivation is a unit. In other words, it is evident that somehow psychological stimulus-response, or S-R Patterns become co-ordinated in the accomplishment of a single purpose. If, for example, an individual is motivated toward the achievement of a college degree, he will integrate all of the diverse patterns of his behavior toward the accomplishment of that end. This involves, in the language of stimulus-response, that he co-ordinates all of his stimulus-response patterns toward the achievement of a single goal.

How are S-R Patterns integrated toward the achievement of a single goal? Do they somehow integrate themselves? Or is there some coordinating activity outside of them, which is not itself an S-R Pattern, an activity which we may call the mind?

Psychologist such as Abraham Maslow believe that there may very well be an ego or a sense of identity which somehow transcends the chain of individual S-R Patterns. In Maslow's vocabulary, this transcending force is known as self-actualisation. The human personality is not, for Maslow, simply a series of programmed resononses to incoming stimuli. The personality, according to Maslow, is capable of initiating its own behavior drawing upon its own resources and by necessarily responding to stimuli from the external world. This is the source of the mind's creativity, its capacity of initiating responses independently of immediate stimuli. The mind is conceived here as an active force which can selectively discriminate from the stimuli of the external world, and be active free choice, respond to some and not to others. What is the source of this capacity? According to Maslow and to all humanistic psychologists, the source of this ability cannot lie within the stimulus-response patterns themselves but in the personality as a whole.

The personality as a whole is a wider unit, which cannot necessarily be reduced to individual stimulus-response patterns.

The attempt to understand the human personality in terms of wider units, of which we can consider humanistic psychology to be one representative, in time became known as the holistic approach to the human personality and to the world surrounding it. Holism, taken from the Greek root, hole, meaning whole, amounts to the claim that it is necessary to understand any given phenomena in any field of endeavor in terms of its surrounding context. The crucial problem, for example, in the area of psychology, for example, would be the problem of how the stimulus-response patterns related to one another in the performance of a single task or in the accomplishment of a single purpose.

Also, in the area of holistic medicine, three questions would be commonly asked:

1. What is the relationship between the individual organs of the body and the organism as a whole?

2. What is the relationship within the organism between mind and body?

3. What is the relationship between the organism and its environment?

The holistic approach to reality stresses entire patterns, whole fields, relationships, rather than small bits and pieces of information. Even contemporary physics is based to a certain degree upon a holistic approach to reality. Even here, the stress of emphasis is placed upon the surrounding field of a sub-atomic particle rather than upon the individual sub-atomic particle. History could be based upon a holistic approach insofar as its attempts to understand the individual in relationship to a wider, surrounding society.

In the fulcrum of contemporary debate, one might consider that there is a far greater chance of conceiving the mind as more than the sum of its behavioral and/or brain activities if one were to adapt a holistic approach to reality instead of one of the possible alternatives, the reductionistic approach. A consistent holist would never reduce the mind to stimulus-response patterns. The mind would always be considered for him as something over and somehow above the individual stimulus-response Patterns. If this were so, could this activity be in any way considered as separate from the brain itself?

It the superiority of the holistic approach could be demonstrated, the distinctiveness of mind and brain might be one of the consequent truths established. But what is the real evidence of the superiority of the holistic approach? We have seen some of the evidence already, namely the defectiveness of the alternative: the defectiveness of reductionism in accounting for the sense of co-ordinated activities in the human personality.

Is it reductionism, as an approach to reality, possibly somehow defective in other ways? It is the insufficiency of the reductionist approach to account for so much of reality that I would now like to direct attention.

Problems for Reductionism

Probably no one better than authors Hofstadter and Dennett in The Mind's Eye have revealed some obstacles which any strictly reductionistic approach to reality must inevitably incur. The major problem confronting any reductionist is always the problem of personal identity. Let us assume that we identify the human personality with the atoms or molecules of the brain or, adapting Skinner's approach, let us claim that we identify human personality with stimulus-response patterns. It follows from this line of reasoning that we must then claim the human individual is nothing more than the sum of his stimulus-response patterns or possibly nothing more than the atoms and molecules which comprise that individual's brain or entire body. Here, she is reunited to her daughter.

As Hofstadter and Dennett well point out, assuming this is the case may not necessarily be the result of scientific sophistication but of a certain lack of scientific imagination. The authors ask us to imagine the case of Sarah's mother, marooned on Mars at some date in the future. Now the technology of that advanced era permits telecloning or the complete cloning or an identical human being over a vast distance. Marooned on Mars, Sarah's mother has no choice but to step into the Tele-clone IV, where her body is dismantled, beamed by way of radio signal back to earth for the construction of a carbon copy, and an identical body with identical memory is constructed and steps forth from the booth on Earth.

The question for us consists of whether we can really consider this identical copy to be, in reality, Sarah's mother. Or did Sarah's mother die on Mars? If the reality of the situation is that Sarah's mother died on Mars, then how can we account for Teleclone V, a later technological breakthrough, which will permit Sarah's mother to remain marooned on Mars without dismantling her body, while her carbon copy is reassembled on earth?

Plainly, in the case of this fictitious, science fiction type example, we are presented with almost insurmountable difficulties if we are to take a position of philosophical materialism or reductionism in regard to the human personality. For we can no longer account for individuality or for what philosophers call personal identity. If the human person is nothing but the sum of the atoms and molecules which comprise him or her, then the individuality or the personal identity of Sarah's mother must change with every change in her atoms and molecules.

Sarah's mother, marooned on Mars can plainly no longer be Sarah's mother as she steps forth from the booth on Earth for in both places, Sarah's mother is comprised of completely different atoms and molecules. Also, her stimulus-response patterns from this moment onwards will undergo change. Yet, intuitively, in both of those cases, many of us would probably assume that Sarah's mother, both as she died on Mars and at the present moment is probably the same woman, the same individual. Yet if we insist upon sticking to the reductionist hypothesis, it seems that we cannot explain how Sarah can be the same woman at those two different moments of her life, since at these two different moments she is comprised of entirely different material elements, i.e., of entirely different atoms and molecules. It is here that we arrive at what seems to many to be the real impasse for reductionism as a scientific credo.

The Mind as Program

Nevertheless, Hofstadter and Dennett, in their latest compilation, propose a way out of this impasse, Neither author wishes to be considered as a reductionist or as a naive materialist. Indeed, they have well pointed to the seeming impossibility of this view. Perhaps, they speculate, the mind could be to a form of "software", like the "software" of a computer. The "software" is the basic program, into which all of the data which the mind processes from the external world are fed into it. The mind is not identical with any particular material embodiment, for the human bodies undergoes a complete cycle of cellular change every seven years, according to many estimates. Should we, pursuing this line of thinking, assume that we become seven different individuals, throughout the course of a normal human lifespan?

Such a conclusion will not be necessary if we steadfastly maintain the proposition that the mind of the individual is to be likened to a form of "software" or "program", which regulates all of these cellular changes. Extrapolating to some degree, it might be possible to consider scientific DNA (the abbreviation for deoxyribonucleic acid), which we inherit from both parents and which directs all of the activity in every individual cell of the human body, as the "software" or "program" of the body. In this consideration, one would not necessarily consider the material elements comprising DNA to be themselves the "software", or alternately the program, but rather, the set of instructions regulating all of the activities of the cell from initial division to death. In the opinion of Hofstadter and Dennett, it is this set of "software" or "programmed" instructions which should be considered as the human mind.

Yet in this conception of the mind as "program" neither Hofstadter nor Dennett seem to think that the mind can possibly be regarded as an entity which could ever exist independently of the brain and central nervous system which it "programs". "Software", for them, can never exist independently of "hardware". But in what sense is this true? Does not the so-called systems and applications "software" continue to exist in computer libraries even if all of the individual computers should through some fatality such as perhaps, severe fire, become destroyed? To believe this would, according to Hofstadter and Dennett, once again commit us to some view of the so-called "ghost-in-the-machine". In their view, the "ghost" can never exist independently of the machine.

In the view of others such as the philosopher, Lucas, who is cited by Hofstadter and Dennett in their book, it definitely can. In Lucas' opinion, the capacity of the mind or soul to maintain independent existence after the moment of death, was one of the implications of a mow famous theorem in contemporary mathematics known as Godel's Theorem, or sometimes the Incompleteness Theorem. The Incompleteness Theorem was a discovery of the contemporary mathematician, Kurt Godel. The basic tenet of this theory amounts to the claim that no system of mathematics can adequately explain its own foundations, at least not within that system. In order to explain the foundations of any given system of mathematics, it will be necessary to go outside of that system into another system which is more inclusive, more comprehensive. In the negative, no system can reflect upon its own foundations. No mathematical system is, so to speak, self-reflective.

But the human mind is self reflective. It is aware of its existence as an individual. It is aware of its activities and can reflect upon these. It can examine and criticize its past motives because it is self-conscious. For the philosopher Lucas, this seemed to prove that the mind was aware of its own foundations, and could reflect upon them. The mind, for Lucas, seemed to transcend the barriers or limitations of Godel's Incompleteness Theorem.

Completely unlike any given system in mathematics, here was a system which really could reflect upon its own foundations. Because the mind could reflect upon its own foundations, this seemed to prove to Lucas that the mind was somehow other than its own foundations. By certain extrapolations, if the mind could reflect upon the activity of the brain, this was proof for Lucas that the mind was somehow other than the brain. It was, in brief, for Lucas, an independently existing entity with the capacity for immortality.

This attempted proof is vigorously combatted by Hofstadter and Dennett. The authors' rebuttal takes the route of the counter-example, or of the example so often employed to prove the opposite case. The authors' counterstand consists in proving that there are many examples of self-reflective system in the physical world. To cite merely one, it is possible for a television set to be self-reflective in the sense of processing or receiving its own image. Locate the TV set in the room of the station which is being transmitted, and its own image will flash upon the screen. Increasingly smaller and smaller images of the TV set will be found to be nested within that interior image, and so on, ad infinitum. In the physical world, this is the exact parallel for Hofstadter and Dennett of self-reflexivity. The thesis of both Hofstadter and Dennett is that if this can occur in the physical world, the same process must also relate to the mind. There is no reason, in their opinion, to believe that simply because the mind can reflect upon its own activity, that it is therefore entitled to the status of a special, independent entity, which can survive the death and dissolution of the body. The mind may not be the sum of atoms and molecules which comprise the brain for Hofstadter and Dennett, but it is not therefore the kind of "software" or "program" which can exist independently of the body. It may be the program of the body, For Hofstadter and Dennett, but it definitely requires the body in order to exist.

Once we divorce or separate the "software" of the brain from the hardware of the "body", we are expressing variations of philosophic dualism and we are definitely outside the scope of both Hofstadter and Dennett's thesis. Because it is possible to conceive of "software" as somehow completely independent of "hardware", the possibility of which we have already imagined, we can see one of the central flaws of this same thesis.

Conclusion: The Image of Mind as Transformer of Psychic Energy

Are physical systems self-reflective in any real sense, as Hofstadter and Dennett imagine them to be? For example, the television set which reflexively transmits a series of increasingly involuted images of itself? Even if we consider the physical realm as on some level parallel with the psychic, do we really possess here a flawless example of a system which somehow reflects upon itself?

Perhaps not. It is entirely possible that we may not even be able to consider the TV set as self-reflective even in the physical realm. The energy on which this set runs if provided by a system which operates outside of its assemblage of tubes and capacitors, and which in some form could exist in complete independence of that box . In addition, the powerful transmitter auditory and visual waves constitutes yet another example of a system which exists independently of the set itself. Most important, the auditory and visual waves sent out by the transmitter exist whether the individual TV set is there to receive them or not. We are daily bombarded with radio and TV waves in any given room. They exist as physical realities, but they are outside the range of our sight and hearing until they are transformed or modulated to that level by the individual radio or TV.

In the final analysis, it is the vibrating undulatory system of visual and auditory waves which makes the nested image of small TV's on the original set and this system could exist independently of the receiving set. As a physical system, it could only be reflective in reference to objects external to itself, either the TV set or of any other elements in the transmitting environment.

Could the human brain be conceived of on a level vaguely analogous to this, not so much as a transmitter but as transformer of the psychic energy of the soul? Unlike a physical system, it would possess the genuine capacity of being self-reflective. But it would operate only upon the individual transforming brain which was receptive to its level of energy. In this way, we distinguish the individual human person, i.e., by that individual's level of receptivity.

In the materialistic, reductionistic heyday of science, speculations such as these could never be entertained. But with the decline of that tradition which many see in the reinstatment of the role of the observer in twentieth century physics and with the inception of humanistic psychology in our century, possibly the science of the future may yet confirm such seeming absurdities. In any event, the thrust of recent science has been to bring it increasingly closer to the borderlands of philosophy. Would it be so outrageous to assume that sometime in the future, the two fields might unite in a common enterprise, the pursuit of the frontiers of reality through the experimental observation of science and philosophy's skeptical questioning of the foundations of our knowledge?

CHAPTER FOUR

THE PROBLEM OF PERSONAL IDENTITY

The problem of personal identity has always been a frequent topic of analysis for philosophers, but especially in recent years. There are many reasons for this. However, the most prominent of these reasons has to do with the empiricist epistemology which many contemporary philosophers have adapted at the outset. If all conceptual knowledge begins in the senses and has an ultimate referent to sensation, to what concrete physical sensations can be refer personal identity?

To what concrete, sensible referent do you owe your personal identity? What distinguishes you as an individual from the person next to you? Does your distinctiveness, your individuality lie in something which is concrete and sensible? Perhaps the mark of your personal identity, of your individuality lies in the atoms and molecules which comprise the brain. The atoms and molecules of your brain differ from the atoms and molecules of the brain of every other individual in the world. Or, extending this, we may wish to claim that the distinguishing feature of personal identity lies in the body. It is the atoms and molecules of your body which distinguish it from the atoms and molecules of the body of everyone else who exists in the world. If you held that personal identity was a matter of the atoms and molecules of the brain, your answers would plainly be in line with what many have interpreted as the findings of modern science, and these findings, again, according to many, have their roots in empiricistic epistemology.

So perhaps it is the body which constitutes the root of personal identity. What distinguishes one person from another is the possession of an individual body, unique and distinct from that of everyone elses. The attempt to locate personal identity in the individual body of a person certainly possesses the appearance of a clear, definite solution to the longstanding problem of personal identity. What could be a more definite solution than that of locating the source of personal identity in humans, animals, and, for that matter, in all plants, in the body itself? The body plainly demarcates any living entity as an individual. Indeed, this solution has often been adapted by many who see in such a solution a mark of scientific sophistication.

Upon first examination, such a solution seems to have no problems attendant upon it. But is this the case? Authors Hofstadter and Dennett, in The Mind's Eye, have pointed out that this kind of solution may not be a mark of scientific sophistication at all, but may point, rather to a lack of scientific imagination. Can the mind really be identified with the body?

In their introduction to The Mind's Eye, authors Hofstadter and Dennett have pointed out many of the difficulties that lie in the wake of identifying the mind with the physical body. It is just some of these difficulties which this author would now like to recount. The upshot may be that we will have to probe elsewhere in our search for the roots of personal identity.

Personal Identity and The Body

Let us pose for reflection the imaginary case which Hofstadter and Dennett in the same introduction to *The Mind's Eye: Fantasies and Reflections on Self and Soul* (New York: Basic Books, 1981), bring to our attention. The setting concerns the future and manned space travel to Mars and judging by the advanced technology presented herein, to all the other planets of the solar system. Sarah's mother's rocket ship has failed to work and she is marooned on Mars, millions of miles away from her eight year old daughter back on Earth. There is no way, after a three year absence, that she can rejoin her daughter back on Earth, at least by normal means, and, finally, in desperation, she steps into Telecom IV. Telecom IV is the postulated latest technological advance in the biological duplication of humans. Sarah's mother, employing the ultimate in technological invention, steps into Telecom IV, which promptly dismantles her body, while flashing coded electronic signals to Earth, on the basis of which reception, Telecom IV on Earth, assembles an identical duplicate of her body with an identical memory. Sarah's mother consequently steps forth from the chamber, exultant at the prospects of rejoining her daughter at last.

Nevertheless, here the perplexity enters. Is this really Sarah's mother? It is this question which the editors of The Mind's Eye, a contemporary compilation of articles dealing with the problem of personal identity, pose to us. If personal identity is to be equated with the body, there is not a single atom or molecule in the body of Sarah's mother present to her on Earth which also existed on Mars. And yet it appears that Sarah's mother on Earth is the same person as Sarah's mother on Mars.

It is at this point that the editors enter upon an even further complication. Consider a somewhat later in date even greater technological breakthrough, the Telecom V. This extraordinary device, the most astounding invention yet devised, will reduplicate Sarah's mother on Earth while allowing the original Sarah's mother on Mars to keep on living. There will be no necessity to dismantle her body. Which of these two individuals is the real mother of the eight year old daughter on Earth? The one on Mars or the one on Earth? Plainly, the seemingly clear-cut solution of assimilating personal identity with the body reveals its inadequacy at this point, if not previously. The editors pose the problem of personal identity in a provacative manner, but leave the solution to our own mental tinkering. This author would like to suggest the possibility of one solution which may imply that the materialistic foundations often inherent in many contemporary scientific worldviews, are completely inadequate as a solution to the problem of personal identity. It may indeed be the case that the foundations of our physical science may require some sharp revisions, hidebound protestors notwithstanding.

One Possible Solution

Personal identity is obviously not reduceable to the body. If it were, we would be left with no alternative but that of claiming that Sarah's mother on Mars and

Sarah's mother on Earth are two different people. This solution plainly flies in the face of our commonsense intuitions. It is, so to speak, counter-intuitive. We desire to claim that the woman of Earth and on Mars are the same individual. But what about Televcom V? How is it possible to claim that it is possible for Sarah's mother to remain living on Mars and still possess the same identity of the woman now living on Earth? Of what does personal identity consist in this strange paradox?

One person cannot obviously inhabit two different bodies. The woman on Earth and on Mars must be two different individuals. Or so it would seem, if we are not to be left with the absurd alternative that the body of the woman on Mars and the body of the woman on Earth both belong to the same individual, which also seems to fly in the face not only of our materialistic worldview but with commonsense as well. For we know that one mind can never inhabit more than one body. It is always the activity of one mind which directs the activity of one body.

But how can we be sure that this is the case? Our commonsensical intuitions seem to merely confirm that this is the case which usually occurs. On the other hand, how are we to understand cases of the so-called dual personality? Or of the so-called split brain patients, in which the two lobes of the brain are cut surgically in extreme cases of epilepsy? In situations such as these, is it possible to claim that somehow two or possibly more personalities reside in the same person?

Such claims, it is true, would flatly contradict certain materialistic worldviews. Nevertheless, if these worldviews are truly as evident and as logical as some would seem to hold, the consequence of all such worldviews would be to claim that the root and source of all personal identity is the body. This we have seen cannot be so, of if the body were the source of individuality, one would be forced to hold that Sarah's mother on Mars and later on Earth were two different people, and this, we plainly think, is not so.

Our solution, if there is to be one, lies in the direction of abandoning all such materialistic worldviews and of claiming, to the contrary, that the body is not the source of personal identity. This negative claim, Hofstadter and Dennett themselves accomplish. Personal identity is not, for them, to be reduced to the atoms and molecules of the brain. The mind, for them, is to be likened to a program, very similar in kind to the "software" of a computer. The "software" is the information system of the computer, and not the box of electrical wiring. "Software" for both of these editors is distinguishable from the body, but not separable from it.

However, the "software" theory of personal identity, put forward by Hofstadter and Dennett itself runs into many problems. One of them is almost unwittingly alluded by Hofstadter and Dennett themselves. This is the problem of the Telecom V. Employing some version of a so called "software" theory of human identity, how can we now explain why it is that if Sarah's mother, the woman on Mars and on Earth, both remain alive, we think that they must now be two very different individuals.

Employing computer language for the sake of argument, we could, of course, claim that the same "software" principle directed the living activities of the body of the woman on Earth and the body of the woman on Mars, both of which bodies, preposterous as it seems, are Sarah's mother, i.e., the same individual, having the same personal identity.

However, the concept of "software" would have to be considered, in this case in terms of perhaps deeper implications. We would no longer conceive of the "software" principle as in any manner of speaking, physical, but we would, to the contrary, have to begin thinking of the same so-called "software" principle as a kind of psychic entity or force, perhaps completely separable from whatever is physical. In this way, we could explain that the psychic realm would somehow be capable of the possession of two bodies, i.e., one individual, Sarah's mother, would be in control and in possession of two bodies, one on Earth and one on Mars. The individual, Sarah's mother, we will conceive of as psychic mind force completely divorceable and separable from the body, indeed, capable of existence without any body at all.

Such is the form of conclusion which Hofstadter and Dennett take pains to avoid, not wanting to be accused of postulating the existence of what we are want to call "ghosts". The existence of spirits, independent of physical existences, appears to be considered by them to be a relic of pre-scientific thought. Nevertheless, the concept of the independent existence of the soul has an ancient and venerable tradition in philosophical Hellenistic thought to support it, the tradition of Plato and Plotinus to which we have already alluded.

The concept of "software", somehow dependent upon existence of the body, embedded in the thinking of Hofstadter and Dennett, does not obviate certain problems, mainly the problem of Telecom V and the simultaneous existence of Sarah's mother in two places, which we have been discussing. Physical "software" must be dependent upon place. All that could be claimed in the case of the Telecom V computer would be that the "software" of the woman on Mars and the "software" of the woman on Earth must somehow be different since "software" in the conception of Hofstadter and Dennett, though not physical, is yet still dependent upon place. Following this line of reasoning, the woman still existing on Mars, a product of Telecom V as well as its other product, the woman now existing on Earth, must somehow be two different women.

However, this form of solution makes no sense whatsoever. If Telecom IV simply geographically relocated Sarah's mother from Mars to Earth, why should the product of Telecom V create two different people? Would it not be much better to more consistently assume that Telecom V, though technologically more advanced, does not constitute a reduplication of life which is, in essence, different from the reduplication of life effected by Telecom IV?

Our more consistent alternative would amount to holding that Sarah's mother, existing both on Earth and on Mars, are the same person. Only now they are dual in location. One person now inhabits two bodies. One mind, one psychic force now attempts to direct the activities of two bodies in different parts of the solar system.

Would such a solution necessarily be as preposterous as it seems? Perhaps not. We could begin to conceive of the mind as a kind of transformer, physically translating psychic energy into physical energy, and also operating in the reverse direction, the kind of image which was elaborated in the previous chapter. Psychic energy, as an independent force, would have no geographical locale, hence it could operate across space and over distances. Perhaps, two persons can be in one body (the dual personality) or that Sarah's mother, as one person, can co-habit two bodies. Such rare occasions may be considered as freaks of nature, which may occur as rarely as that two parties are accidentally placed on the same telephone line, for the reception and transmission of messages. Perhaps psychic lines are at times subject to such disorders.

It is possible to call for support of such seemingly patent absurdities, certain strains in contemporary physics. The oft cited Einstein-Podolosky-Rosen experiment in physics has produced much peculiar phenomena which is engaging the attention and the propounding of theories by some in the scientific community. From vast physical distances, it is possible to produce similar patterns of behavior from small electrically charged sub-atomic particles known as photons. The photons, once in physical proximity to one another are now separated physically. Change the spin either to the right or the left on one photon, and the spin of the other photon will proceed in the same direction.

What could possibly account for this seeming magnetism over a distance? Could one photon be signalling the other? If so, the signal would have to travel faster than the speed of light, which violates known physical laws, though some nevertheless think that this may be the real explanation. Or, there may be an underlying connectiveness or unity in Nature which transcends physical distance.

If either of these possibilities are true, one can see that the possibility of similar phenomena operating over distances is something which even our contemporary physics can entertain as theory. Why may not psychic phenomena transcend distance in a similar manner, one mind or psychic force controlling different bodies over vast distances? Psychic force could in this manner of speaking be conceived of as transcending space, transcending distance.

Control problems, of course might present themselves. One mind, two bodies across vast distances may appear to the mind of the possessor like a confusing telephone line in which two parties are simultaneously conducting a conversation, simultaneously transmitting and receiving messsages, which are often in conflict. Yet this may be one of the problems caused by personal identity when it results in such rare, freak applications. Yet such freaks of nature may well account for the phenomena of dual personalities.

Personal identity is, indeed, a problem; in some respects it may be akin to a mystery. How can one person inhabit two bodies? Or two persons, one body. Yet if we do not allow for the possibility of such strange phenomena, we are once again saddled with the solution that it is the body, the individual body which constitutes personal identity. This solution, in turn, inaugurates more problems than it can possibly solve. Such a solution could never solve problems in the imaginable future, such as the Telecom IV and the Telecom V teleporters. It could never solve problems which man may increasingly encounter as his exploration of the universe and the base of his knowledge continue to broaden. Perhaps this is because reality is not merely restricted to the physical, and even our contemporary physics is beginning to understand this. Perhaps, the mind can exist independently of the body, and this is, perhaps, the solution to the problem of personal identity. One mind, two or several bodies; one body, two or more minds, may not be such a paradox in this non-physicalistic perspective.

PART THREE

REFLECTION S

CHAPTER FIVE

DIMENSIONS

Is what we call reality exhausted by its physical dimensions? Is the physical world entirely circumscribed by length, width, and height? According to Einstein's Special Theory of Relativity, we would have to add the dimension of time to this list, for time is often considered as a Fourth Dimension in contemporary physics, a dimension in addition to length, width, and height. Mathematicians have never found any sufficient reason why the dimensions of reality, even the physical dimensions of reality should be comprised of just three.

Euclidean geometry, the geometry invented, of course by Euclid, in the ancient world, operates within the plain of two dimensions, length and width, i.e., with the objects which could be fitted onto any two dimensional plane. Solid geometry deals with physical objects which exist within a three dimensional plane. It was not until the nineteenth century that mathematicians began to plainly recognize the insufficiency of Euclidean geometry. Geometry was capable of operating upon quite other axioms than those which were devised by Euclid. The mathematicians Riemann, Lobachevsky and Bolyai, independently elaborated geometries operating upon other axioms, the geometries of a fourth and fifth dimension. Theoretically, there is no reason why there cannot exist an infinite number of dimensions— geometrical dimensions proliferating into infinity.

Indeed, the Special and the General Theories of Relativity were constructed on the basis of a four dimensional geometry. The question which we might ask pertains to whether it is possible to construct other theories on the basis of geometries of higher dimensions. Already, the science of quantum mechanics is dealing with many dimensional levels of subatomic particles. Mathematical physics is the new avenue of exploration, and the hope is that it may be able to solve many contemporary problems and enigmas of the physical universe. Perhaps mathematical physics will be the new tool in exploring the geometries of higher dimensions.

But what could be the nature of these dimensions? Would it be possible to describe them in physical terms? Finally, how is it that we would be willing to define a dimension?

Let us begin by considering that a dimension could be defined as an entity capable of division into parts. The line, for example, as a one dimensional figure, could be divided into points. Any plane figures, in turn, could be partitioned into lines. The three dimensional solid, in turn, could be also divided or partitioned into the parts of various planes. Time, considered as a fourth dimension, could be divided into its various, relative moments.

It appears that the physical world which we know can be considered according to its spatial and temporal features. Any physical object which we can recognize takes up space in a place or position of three dimensions and occupies a finite existence within a limited time span. Is it possible that we can legitimately speak of the physical world in reference to dimensions which are neither spatial nor temporal?

The philosopher, Immanuel Kant, in the eighteenth century, considered that space and time were merely features of the mind's structural apparatus through which it perceived the world. The world perceived through space and time merely presented to us the realm of things-as-they-appear-to-us, and not the realm of things as they are in themselves. The realm of things in themselves was neither spatial nor temporal.

Since there is no necessity, according to many mathematicians, of perceiving the world as limited to three dimensions, it may be possible that space and time are a part of the cognitive, limiting apparatus through which we perceive the world. It may be we ourselves who structure the world in a three dimensional manner. But, nevertheless, the number of possible dimensions is theoretically infinite. It is precisely this realm of theoretically infinite dimensions that Kant may have been referring to when he addressed himself to the realm of things-in-themselves. Whether this interpretation is indeed a sound one or rather the result of the process of reading too much into Kant, it is nevertheless plausible that the realm of reality itself, the realm of things-in-themselves, may belong to a possibly infinite number of dimensions, of which we are cognizant of merely three because of the blinders which our minds have placed upon the perceiving apparatus. Hence, limited to this world, we partition it into many different parts, according to various points in space and time.

It is possible to partition the world of space and time in both a spatial and a temporal direction, but would it nevertheless be possible to consider any possible dimension as divisible into parts in the same sense? How could any dimension which is not spatial and not temporal be divisible into parts? To begin with, how could we even imagine such a dimension, limited as we are by our three-dimensional apparatus?

Previously, a dimension was defined as any entity capable of division into parts. We can easily imagine physical and temporal parts in the physical world, but is it nevertheless possible to refer to an entity as something which is comprised of parts, even if these parts are not either spatial or temporal parts? The answer to this question might be a qualified yes. The divisions of wholes into parts which are neither spatial nor temporal seems to prevail throughout the entire realm of mathematics. For example, it is possible to divide a theorem in geometry into many parts or steps. All of the steps are distinguishable from the others but none of them is plainly separable from any of the others. None of the steps could be considered as, in any sense, physical, separable apart of the entire theorem of geometry. Some parts are mentally distinguishable, but not necessary physically separable.

The example of geometry was chosen in this case. However, what has been said in reference to geometry is even truer in branches of mathematics which are more abstract. In algebra, it is possible to separate one unknown from another. In calculus, it remains possible to separate one part of a theorem from another. Nevertheless, in neither of these cases is it true that any of the parts which we distinguish amounts to a physical division.

Perhaps distinctions will not amount to divisions in the realm of other dimensions. Indeed, physical division and separability may belong only to the realm of the three (or should one include time as the fourth?) dimensions with which we are acquainted. In the entire realm of mathematics, it is so frequently possible to distinguish objects which we cannot physically separate. What is true of mathematics is also true of the world of contemporary sub-atomic particle physics. In the view of philosopher of science, Milek Capek, in *The Philosophic Impact of Contemporary Physics*, if the profoundly revolutionary implications of Relativity and Quantum Mechanics are ever fully realized, it will be seen that space, time, matter, motion, energy, and causality are no longer the discrete, separable units which they were envisioned to be in nineteenth century science, but that rather the boundary line between them now seems to be more difficult to decide. In brief, space, time, motion, matter, energy, and causality, are distinguishable but not separable.

Might these more abstract, philosophical implications hold true because contemporary particle physics deals, at least in part, with many different dimensions? The physicist, operating in the quantum realm, already employs equations which treat of four or five or six dimensions. It is possible that any of these dimensions might be defined as having parts, which are distinguishable from one another, though not physically separable, like steps in theorems of geometry, or, more abstractly, like the unknowns in any mathematical equation.

If this is the case, in treating of these unknown dimensions, we need not abandon our original definition of a dimension as an entity which possesses parts. The unknown dimension, here, still possesses parts, only the parts are not physical and separable, but rather distinguishable like parts of a mathematical equation. Again, the number of such dimensions is theoretically infinite.

What would be the characteristics of such dimensions? Certainly, without direct knowledge of these, how would it be possible to enter descriptions of them? Let us begin, so to speak, negatively, with the negative definition. Such dimensions would not be physical. They would not be spatial and they would not be temporal. If such dimensions as entities having parts possess real existence, are we familiar with anything like this?

We have familiarity with the realm of other dimensions, and yet this familiarity may relate more to the realm of inner space. All of us are, at least to some extent, aware of the realm of our internal psyches. We are also aware of the realm of abstract concepts, concepts relating to seemingly changeless norms in the moral world and also to pure mathematics. None of these realms are physical, yet they have parts. They also influence the physical world. The mind is an effective agent in healing or slaying the body as was reported by Pelletier in the Bible of holistic medicine, *The Mind As Healer: The Mind As Slayer*. The correct or possibly, incorrect mathematical equations are the mental instruments which an engineer employs in the construction of a bridge. We could imagine these different realms as somehow interactive, as metaphorically nested within one another as the first two dimensions are nested within the third, and so on, ad infinitum.

Such dimensions would not be physical yet they would nevertheless contain the complexity of many parts. There is a certain degree of evidence from at least two dimensions of contemporary science that such dimensions may exist: the area of the so-called "black hole" physics, and the area of recent investigations into psychic phenomena. I now like to consider each of these areas of investigation in turn.

Consider the recent, exciting discovery of twentieth century science, the detection of the so-called "black hole" by balloon with X-Ray detecting equipment in the area of Cygnus the Swan. A "black hole" is one of the most intriguing objects in modern astronomy. It is the death throes of a star which has undergone the final process of ageing. Stars, like all living organisms, from the smallest one celled animal to man to the giant whale, undergo a process of ageing and death. A star, astronomers tell us, is nothing but one giant thermonuclear reaction. In the process of emitting energy, stars age. From the time of early youth as young, hot blue stars, all stars eventually mature in the timespan of several millions of years into yellow stars and then into "red giants", stars which are blowing their stacks, so to speak, with thermonuclear reaction energy. After the passage of several more million years, stars in old age collapse with gravitational force in successive stages into smaller white stars, the size of the Earth, and then into "neutron stars", no larger than New York City, and sometimes they seem to disappear under the force of their own gravity into nothingness, or into what is often known as a "black hole".

Strange phenomena await any visitor or inanimate object caught within the gravitational force of a so-called "black hole". Following the contemporary science of Einstein's Theory of Special Relativity, the object shrinks to nothing in space and time, for it, after dilating or slowing by stages, eventually ceases to exist for it. Here, in a unique and peculiar mode of existence known as the "singularity", time and space no longer exist. This, then, may be referred to as the dimension of reality which is "beyond space-time". Yet there seems to be some evidence that certain physical reactions of the universe finally enter the "black hole" stage. "Black holes" may indeed exist in the center of many galaxies which appear to be collapsing, being devoured in stages by a monstrous "black hole" in the center.

Is it possible to equate the singularity with the psychic realm? The "psychic" is, in some sense, beyond both space and time. Consider the internal life of the mind. Are elation and depression located within specified, concrete place and time? Or, are most human moods and sentiments all-pervasive? Here, in "singularity", we may have encountered the next of the dimensions known to man, the realm of the psychic. Psychic moods have parts and behavioral features and attributes which are often described, yet none of these are either physical nor separable.

Nevertheless, it is the psychic realm which is capable of influencing the physical realm. The mind conditions the body as well as, in many cases, the physical environment surrounding it. We manipulate and change our bodies as well as the external environment. Must we make the assumption that our ability to do so begins and ends with our individual bodies? All of which discussion brings us to the topic of current research into psychic phenomena. There is some empirical evidence, coming from this field that the mind's ability to alter the physical world of matter may not be limited to the body of the individual. Current research suggests the possibility that the mind may have the power to alter the position and location of objects through a power known as psychokinesis. Also, the same body may possess the power of changing its location in oft reported out of the body experiences, essentially the psychic phenomena known as teleportation.

Research along these lines plainly points to the possibility of the existence of a completely separate psychic realm or dimension, a broader realm in which spatial and temporal dimensions are nested. It is this realm which could explain the power of the mind to act over vast distances, such phenomena as are reputed to take place in psychokinesis and teleportation.

It is the psychic dimension which could account for such weird phenomena as the previously alluded to Einstein-Podalsky-Rosen Experiment. Particles which exhibit similar behavior over vast distances could be responding to the presence of a broader psychic dimension in which they are nested, somewhat analogous to the manner in which by twisting a three dimensional compass one could create a motion of two similar curves at opposite ends of a paper lying on a two-dimensional plane.

We may live in a nested universe, and, it is this concept of the universe which is, in actuality, an ancient tradition. It has been held by every neo-Platonic philosopher, in some version, during the early centuries of the Christian Church. In the version given form in the Enneads of Plotinus, from the One, emenated the Nous of Intelligence, with its logoi spermatakoi or seed of Reason. The "logoi spermatakoi" were distinguishable but not separable from one another. From the Nous, emanated the World Soul, the Demiurge of the visible world, and from the World Soul, the visible world of our acquaintance.

The World Soul of Plotinus is the realm of the intelligence, the realm of the separated psychic. The Nous was the realm of the separated, existing ideas, the realm of the Platonic Ideas. Beyond Nous, there was the One, nameless, ineffable. From the vantage point of a more contemporary understanding which has dealt with four dimensional space-time, the realm beyond these dimensions may be the dimension of the psychic, beyond this the dimension of abstract physical and ethical laws, and beyond this, the dimension of Yogic meditation. This amounts to the thesis that we may live in a tiered, nested, hierarchical universe and that our contemporary science may one day prove this. Our current science is hidebound, living upon images and forms of reasoning borrowed from the Newtonian science of the nineteenth century. For such a science, there is no hierarchical universe, no dimensions beyond the three physical dimensions which lie directly ahead.

CHAPTER SIX

SPACE-TIME AND SPINOZA

Controversy concerning the real nature of space and time is long standing in the history of philosophy, dating back to Plato, who considered space in his dialogue, Timaeus, as the "Receptacle". Like many of the other enduring controversies in Philosophy, the lengthy debate concerning what space and time really are has never yielded a solution satisfactory to the entire philosophical community. Nevertheless, this space-and-time controversy is of inestimable importance as are the various reasonings that have been postulated as solutions because the entire topic has ramifications in a number of far-ranging fields. Within Philosophy itself Epistemology and the Philosophy of Science would benefit enormously on the finding of a satisfactory working solution to the problem. Additionally, many models of the universe often include within their foundations certain concepts of the nature of both space and time.

Consideration of the problem of time and space is fascinating for yet another reason. Since both time and space are so very closely related to all of human experience perhaps this debate, concerning the real nature of time and space is subject to eventual resolution, at least in principle, through the usage of a combination of commonsensical observations, logic and scientific research. The purpose of this paper is an attempt to combine ordinary observation, logic and the scientific research culled from Newton's Principia and Einstein's Relativity to provide one possible solution to the problem of the real nature of space and time. Even if the solution proves not to be correct, an important gain has been made. A sound manageable method would have been employed in attempting the solution that may in the future prove to be the way in which to achieve its resolution.

Indeed, any correct solution to this problem would be linked to many issues in Epistemology, e.g., the problem of the limits of man's knowledge of the universe. The related question here is whether space and time are only the limiting structures through which man perceives the universe - or, are they realities in themselves? In Epistemology, the problem of space and time is also related to the problem of universals. Are space and time real entities in the external universe? Are they relations between objects - or, are they simply a part of the cognitive structure?

The twin problems of universals and the possible limits of man's knowledge are problems in Epistemology, but they have bearing also upon some of the often discussed problems in the Philosophy of Science. Are the entities and laws that are dealt with in science, realities in themselves - or, simply the limiting structures of the cognitive apparatus through which the world is perceived? Are the space-time fields on which investigation is centered in contemporary physics real entities in the external universe, or more simply a relationship between space-time curvatures?

Are they also part of man's psychological, cognitive apparatus through which he views the world? For philosophers of Science, one of the most controversial problems in contemporary science is the questioning of whether science approximates to the truth of the real, external world - or is it simply an instrument of man's cognitive apparatus, providing information concerning that external world only in the form of meter-readings. Which, of course, is merely to restate the ongoing debate between the Realists and the Anti-realists philosophers working in Philosophy of Science.

If the viewpoint is accepted that space-and-time are real, i.e., that both are somehow entities independent of man's cognition of space and time, then it might be possible also to argue that science, which deals with space and time, give us real knowledge of the physical world and the universe, independently of man's cognition. The "wave function" in quantum mechanics suggest that this is so. In fact, the "Many-Worlds Interpretation" of quantum mechanics holds to the existence of many worlds, operating simultaneously, some with similar, others with different physical laws. This speculation bears similarity to that speculative, metaphysical view of the universe postulated in Spinoza's Ethics, according to which the universe is comprised of only one substance, manifesting itself in many modes, two of which are thought and extension.

The purposes of this paper are twofold. First, to introduce evidence that the space-time matrix is a reality independent of man's cognition of it, an entity that may be considered as having some resemblance to a mode, one of many modes, each having very different matrixes, that, taken collectively are the expressions or manifestations of an underlying "substance". All modes are real, i.e., taken collectively with their attributes, (in a particular mode of extension that contains the attributes of the space-time matrix - namely: four dimensions), modes exist without relying upon human cognition for their existence. Second, to employ a method of arriving at these conclusions that is close to man's experience: Empirical observation, reflective reasoning and scientific findings concerning space and time.

After beginning with a brief sketch of the controversy regarding space and time in the history of philosophy, this paper will be concerned with the implications of this controversy for Epistemology and the Philosophy of Science. Followed by the posing of a Realistic solution to the controversy, referring to the work of one well-known philosopher of science, Hilary Putnam and next, offering additional evidence in support of Dr. Putnam's solution from this writer's own reflections. Finally, the consequences will be detailed by adoption of a Realistic view concerning space and time for Epistemology, and related Philosophy of Science with its attendant model of the universe, somewhat akin to the Substance-Mode universe of Spinoza. The final outcome is that an analysis of space and time carries evidence for the view that man lives not in a single universe, operating under uniform laws everywhere, but in a many modal pluriverse, each mode of which operates under different laws.

PART 1

BRIEF SKETCH OF THE CONTROVERSY

The questions of what are space and time have intrigued man for centuries. Yet, St. Augustine's oft quoted statement with reference to time has a familiarly affecting ring: "What is time? If no one asks me, I know. If someone were to ask the question, I know not" Concerning space and time, philosophers have often queried whether these entities belong to the external world - or, are they in some sense, mental constructs. It is a commonplace observation that space is measured by either rulers or rods and that time is measured by either a sun dial or clocks. Both space and time seem to require the human observer. Can they exist without man? If they can, then in what sense are they real? If they cannot, then how can geological time be considered in which an event took place without the cognizance and participation of man? The controversy concerning the nature of space and of time, with its attendant problems and position statements, will now be reviewed.

a) The Position of the Realist

In the Dialogue, the Timaeus, of Plato, space is assigned a relatively significant ontological status. It is the "Receptacle", the Void. It was from the Receptacle that the Demiurge of the world formed all of the pre-existent geometrical forms or models upon which the presently existing world was based. Space, in this conception, did not depend upon matter for its existence. It was, at least from some perspectives, an independently existing substance. Plato made no essential distinction between space and matter; matter was a form of space, participating in certain pre-existent Forms or Ideas, molded into geometrical models.

The position of Rene Descartes in the seventeenth century was, in many ways, similar. Res Cogitans, (the thinking thing) and Res Extense (the extended thing or space), were both substances, having an independent existence by definition. Matter was merely a mode of extension, or of space. The position that space and time are both substances may, indeed, have been inherited by Isaac Newton in the seventeenth century and by his disciples into the late nineteenth century. The Newtonian position, stated in the more metaphysical portion of the Principa in 1687, has become almost proverbial. Here, Isaac Newton, rebutting the opinion of the so-called "vulgar", asserted that both space and time were eternal attributes, inherent in the mind of the Supreme Being, whether apprehended by human cognition or not. To Newton's disciples, the Newtonians of nineteenth century science, this became known as the position of Absolute Time and Space. Time and space were homogeneous, and time followed uniformly from past to present to future. The view of Absolute Time and Space constituted the foundation and reference point of physical science in the nineteenth century.

b) The counter-proposal of the Moderate Realist

The position with regard to space and time traces back to Aristotle. It amounted to what essentially Newton would have considered to be the opinion of the "vulgar". In his Physics, Aristotle subjected the conception of Space and Time to close analysis, concluding that Space was not the independently existing "Receptacle" of Plato, but rather "the measure of extension", and extension was simply the accident of relation between bodies or the measure of a place of a given body. This was the view, in essence maintained by Liebniz, in the seventeenth century in his famous correspondence with Clarke, an adherent of Newton. Clarke maintains the Realist position that Space was an attribute of the mind of God, whereas Leibniz defends the position that Space was simply a form of relationship between objects. Many scientists and philosophers of science consider that the Special and General Theories of Relativity as put forward by Einstein constitute refutation of the Newtonian conception of Absolute Space - and, in the opinion of Milek Capek, Relativity Theory forces both scientists and philosophers to view both space and time as interrelated and also to understand the space-time matrix of fourth dimensional geometry as simply a relationship between objects. Time, similarly, is considered to be simply a measure of motion. Hence, in the twentieth century, much empirical evidence has been brought to bear upon the proposition that both space and time do not possess independent existence but are rather the measure of relationships between bodies and the measure of motion.

c) Kant's Viewpoint

Kant, in the eighteenth century, was an heir to the Newtonian view of the physical world, but he rejected the conception of space and time as "substances". For Kant, it was the mind that provided the framework of Euclidean Space and Time. Space and time were a part of the inherent structure, the form of intuition, which it imposed on the external world, and without which it would be impossible for the mind to apprehend or organize its experience of things-in-themselves, the noumena, of the external world. For Kant, space and time were necessary, or a priori intuitions. Kan decisively rejected all other positions concerning the nature of space and time.

Space and time could not be concepts of relationships and space and time could not be substances, for if either of these positions were true, certain absurdities would result. First, consider the counter-position that space is a concept. Any concept, in the thinking of Kant must contain divisions, elements or parts, but space does not. Any part of space is homogeneous with the whole of space as can be readily understood when space is imagined behind closed eyelids. Similarly, any segment of time is homogeneous with the whole of time since time flows uniformly. In Kant's conclusion, space and time could not be considered as simply man's concept of the relationships between objects or intervals, but rather because of their homogeneity, they were to be viewed as intuitions.

How could Kant successfully rule out the possibility that space and time were substances, the view of Newton and Clarke? In the "Transcendental Dialectic" of his Critique, Kant relates how this view would lead to antinomies, or paradoxes, relating to the successful attempt to prove opposite positions with regard to the nature of the world, if space and time are considered to be substances. Employing the substance view of space and time, it becomes possible to successively prove that the world both had a beginning in space and that it did not have a beginning in space and time. The argument for a definite beginning is provided by the logical possibility of arriving at the present moment by postulating a definite beginning at some finitely distant moment in the past. Contrariwise, the argument for no definite beginning is provided by the logical possibility of always being able to intuitively imagine a space and time somehow existent before that beginning. The patent absurdity of being capable of logically supporting two diametrically opposed positions, of running into antinomies, proved to Kant that it was impossible to maintain the view of Newton and Clarke that space and time were independently existing substances, and to hold instead that they were part of the structure of the mind through which the mind organized the "manifold of experience." Antinomies were the product of pure reason's attempt to transcend the limits of the mind's inherent structure, part of which were the forms of intuition: Space and time. For Kant, the mind perceived objects in three dimensional Euclidean geometry and in time. Does the four dimensional matrix of space-time in contemporary Relativity Theory prove Kant wrong in his assessment? Not necessarily, because it is still possible that man's commonsensical perceptions of space and time as separate entities is still a product of inherent mental frameworks, the forms of intuitions.

d) The Nominalist Perspective

The Nominalist position veers even more sharply to the position of Kant, and has confined space and time to the mind. For empirically-minded philosophers, such as Locke, Hume and Hodges, space and time are simply names for concepts that arise through man's manner of simplifying relationships between sensations and images. Apart from the mind's ability to associate these, space and time have external, independent existence. Some scientists and philosophers of science think that wither this empiricistic view of the nature of space and time - or, a version of Moderate Realism, amounting to the claim that space and time are relationships between objects, is supported by Relativity Theory.

PART 2

IMPLICATIONS FOR EPISTEMOLOGY

Alternative positions concerning space and time may be the key to many other important problems in philosophy. Many problems in the Theory of Knowledge, such as the problem of universals and the problem of the limitations of man's knowledge would be more amenable to solution were the problems relating to space and time solved first.

a) The Problem Of Universals As Linked To Views Concerning Space and Time

What are space and time? Are they independent substances; relations between objects - or, on the other hand, are they part of the mind's inherent structure; or even concepts associating sensations? Man's notions concerning space and time will condition his thinking relevant to universals.

If space and time are substances, perhaps they themselves are universals, existing independently of the mind. If space and time are a part of the mind's structure, then both could be compared to the status of the "universal" as a concept inherent in the mind. The Kantian position, regarding space and time, leads to the position of conceptualism with reference to the status of the "universal. If, on the other hand, space and time have independent existence, then perhaps they are independently existing Universals, especially if they are to be considered part of the space-time field. The Traditionalistic position, holding that the Universal is completely independent in its existence, independent of the existence of the object is the Epistemological position of "Absolute Realism". Perspectives concerning Space and time will, therefore, strongly condition whether the individual philosopher is an Absolute Realist or a Conceptualist with reference to his position on the status of the Universal.

Also, the Epistemological positions of "Moderate Realism" and of "Nominalism" with reference to Universals is linked to views concerning the nature of both Space and Time. If the position of Aristotle and Leibniz is taken with regard to space and time, i.e., if they are considered simply as relations, the respective measures of place and motion, then space and time are liable to be construed as concepts that are abstracted from things. There follows a strong tendency to be a "Moderate Realist" with reference to the position chosen in relationship to Universals. The Universal will be considered to be a product of abstraction from the thing. Finally, the position whereby space and time are considered to be merely a relation between sensations often culminates in Epistemological Nominalism with reference to Universals, and operating from this perspective, the Universal will be viewed as an even more arbitrary product of the mind's cognition.

Epistemological positions with reference to Absolute or Moderate Realism, Conceptualism, and Nominalism, may have as foundations what is taken to be the nature of Space and Time. If so, proving positions with regard to Space and Time then may be relatively earlier than attempting to prove positions regarding the status of Universals because perspectives on Space and Time may be based upon both observation and current scientific research. Positions concerning Universals cannot be proved in like manner.

b) Space-Time and The Limits of Man's Knowledge

Positions taken anent Space and Time are also the positions taken regarding the natural limits of man's knowledge of the universe. If Space and Time are mental strictures, either in the Kantian or in the Nominalist sense, natural limits on man's ability to know reality will be imposed. For Kant, Space and Time did, indeed, pose such limits on man's cognitive understanding. These so-called "forms of intuition", together with the categories, confined the cognition of the ration being to things-as-they-appear, to phenomena. Space and Time served as structures, along with the categories, on man's knowledge of noumena, or things-in-themselves, rendering them forever inaccessible to human cognition. A similar statement may be made concerning the Nominalistic position regarding Space and Time. For the Nominalist, man's knowledge of the natural universe is confined to phenomena, and Space and Time are themselves phenomena; being merely concepts for arbitrary relationships between sensations.

The Absolute and Moderate Realist position regarding both Space and Time are based on a very different perspective in relationship to man's cognitive capacity to know the real world. Operating within either position, Space and Time are somehow real. For the Absolute Realist, Space and Time exist independently of both the mind and of things in the external universe. For the Moderate Realist, Space and Time exist independently of the mind, but are also real relations, dependent on the existence of things in the external world. Neither of these positions limits man's cognitive capacity to the degree in which strictures and limits are placed upon this capacity for the Conceptualist and the Nominalist. For both the Absolute and the Moderate Realist, Space and Time do not serve as strictures or limits on man's ability to understand things-in-themselves, the noumena of Kantian vocabulary.

Is Man's cognitive capacity fitted simply for phenomena to comprehend the way things appear filtered through the mental strictures of Space and Time, or, can man's cognitive capacity have a cognitive understanding of the noumena, of things-in-themselves, or substances? The problems of Space and Time are intimately connected to problems concerning the limits of man's knowlege and these problems also have direct bearing upon how man conceives reality and the natural universe in his Philosophy of Science.

c) Realism and Anti-Realism in the Philosophy of Science

The Realist in his Philosophy of Science claims that science is an activity which yields "increasing approximations towards the truth", in regard to man's knowledge of Reality. The Anti-Realist, in the philosophy of science, is, however, often an instrumentalist. He holds that theories in Science are, to some degree, "useful fictions" because the theories somehow relate diverse bodies of information into a coherent whole and produce workable results in terms of being able to make successful predictions, but in no sense do they explain or describe the real nature of the physical universe.

Is the physical universe really comprised of submicroscopic particles called atoms? For the Realist, this theory is, at least, an approximation to the truth. For the Instrumentalist or Anti-Realist, this theory is simply useful in balancing chemical equations as a kind of shorthand notation in explaining tracks in cloud chambers, in running nuclear reactors; or, for that matter in the manufacturing of the atomic bombs.

Once again, the dichotomy in the positions of both Realist and Anti-Realist in the Philosophy of Science may often hinge upon prior assumptions in reference to both Space and time. Ideally, tracing both of these positions back to their foundations in regard to time and space may turn out to be one of the most effective ways of settling the controversy between Realist and Anti-Realist.

All of the natural objects which collectively form the topic of study of the sciences are phenomena which are located within space and time. Consequently, the reality or unreality of these theories depend upon prior views concerning space and time. Are space and time somehow real or are they simply constructs of the mind? If space and time are somehow real, if, in the vocabulary of contemporary physics, the space-time field has an independent existence and constitutes itself the new Absolute of contemporary physics, then theories based upon the space-time field have a foundation in the external world of things-in-themselves. If, on the other hand, even the space-time field is somehow a mental construct, then, similarly, all theories based upon this space-time field are mental constructs, and once again there is the opposition between Realism and Anti-Realism or Instrumentalism in the Philosophy of Science.

A "Realistic" position concerning Space and Time will often lead to Realistic views concerning the roe of scientific theories; whereas, a position tending to describe both Space and Time as mental constructs will often culminate in Instrumentallistic or Anti-Realists conceptions of the status of theories in science. The view of Space and Time as mental constructs will sometimes be the foundation for these conceptions of theories in science as having merely the status of mental constructs imposed upon the external world, and serving merely the Instrumentalistic purpose of meter-reading. The real content of the meter-reading remains an unknown.

PART 3

POSSIBLE SOLUTIONS

A purpose of this paper is to argue for a Realist solution to the problem of the nature of Space and Time. Support for this purpose was found in the writings of Hilary Putnam. In his book, Mathematics: Matter & Method (1975) and especially in his article, "An Examination of Grunbaum's Philosophy of Geometry" Putnam maintains a Realist position. After presenting Putnam's position, this writer should like to draw upon some personal observations tending to support Putnam's realistic, substance view of the nature of the space-time field.

a) Putnam's Solution

Putnam holds that space-time is real, namely that it has an existence independent of either human cognition or of the relationships between the particles of matter contained within it. This view appears reasonable since contemporary physics has demonstrated that what is called "matter" is simply a curvature in the pre-existent space-time field. In this interpretation, matter is simply a perturbation, in what otherwise is an essentially homogeneous field: the field of space-time. As both Relativity theory and Quantum Mechanics reveal, matter and space are interrelated with only a subtle distinction between them.

According to Putnam (See: "Examination of Grunbaum's Philosophy of Geometry") Einstein, himself, returned to a version of the nineteenth century postulate of an "ether", the supposed medium in which light waves propagated somewhat in a manner in which sound waves propogate in the medium of the air. In his later years, Einstein claimed that the gravitational field comprised of space-time, was the "true ether", and like the repudiated "ether" of the Michelson-Morley experiment for determining an "ether drag", the gravitational field serves the purpose of an "Absolute". Like the ether it is homogeneous subject only to the perturbations of the curvature of matter.

The Michelson-Morley experiment, performed in 1892, was an attempt to determine the speed of light when it travelled in a direction against that of its natural medium, the ether. If light travelled in a medium as sound travelled in air, then the speed of light should be retarded in a direction against that medium as the speed of sound would be similarly retarded when it travelled in a direction opposite to that of the surrounding wind. This famous experiment with mirrors and a light source failed to detect any such retardation. As a result of the failure, Einstein postulated that the speed of light is always a constant, always roughly 186,000 m.p.'s relative to the velocity of the observer. Q.E.D.: Light did not travel in an ether.

With the collapse of the theory of "the ether" came repudiation of Isaac Newton and his disciples with the nineteenth century's theory of inertial or privileged frames of reference with respect to the "ether", the theory of Absolute Space and Absolute Time. Henceforth, scientists and philosophers of science began to consider space and time as relative. Time came to be considered the measure of motion, or change in position between two objects, and space came to be considered the measure of distance between any two objects. The newer position was discovered by Milec Capek in his, The Philosophic Impact of Contemporary Physics, to be a revival of the earlier Aristoteliean position in regard to space and time. Space, no longer maintaining a privileged position becomes simply "place", a relationship between objects, and time becomes once again simply the "measure of motion".

Putnam states, however, the philosophic concept of a universal ether was never repudiated, even if the physical concept of a "light ether" was. Hence, the Michelson-Morley Experiment in disproving the existence of "light ether" laid the foundation for the space-time matrix of the gravitational field in Relativity Theory. The gravitational field, however, is still an "Absolute", according to Putnam, and also according to Einstein, because it is homogeneous. Within it, are contained all the space-time warps of what are perceived as ordinary matter. The gravitational field within space-time is the new constant, or Absolute because it is the same for all observers.

Newton was right about "Absolute" Space and Time, argues Putnam, at least, on the philosophic level. His error lay in physical theory, i.e., in not anticipating the gravitational space-time field of twentieth-century physics and instead postulating the universal existence of a "force of gravity".

Nevertheless, space-time is not merely a set of formalized relationships between objects. It is rather an independent substance. This position can be partially proven, according to Putnam, by examining the manner in which mankind thinks of ordinary universal standards of length, such as the platinum-irridium bar, which will neither expand or contract with temperature changes. Yet, it is possible physically to subject the platinum-irridium bar to temperatures so high that it will expand, i.e., speaking of atomic/nuclear ranges of heat, so high it would expand to twice its normal length. Would the standard foot now be twice as long? No, because according to Putnam's article, "An Examination of Grunbaum's Philosophy of Geometry", the standard still maintains a relationship to an absolute extension, which is a feature of the absolute space-time field. Hence, space-time is the new, independently existing frame of reference.

b) Additional Evidence for Putnam's Solution

It seems to this writer that Putnam is essentially correct in his contention with relation to the nature of the space-time gravitational field. For him it does exist independently of both so-called material objects and that of man's cognition of it. Space-time is the new "ether" of twentieth century physics; matter is simply a warp in the homogeneity of space-time. The example of the platinum-irridium bar can be used in support of this hypothesis. Several other examples from this writer's personal reflection could be brought forward to marshall evidence in support of Putnam's position.

Consider the following two examples. First, consider employing a completely hypothetical mechanical clock which operates on an irregular basis because of periodic failures in the springs of its mechanisms... and employ the imaginary construct that it is the only object now extant in the physical universe. For a period of a hundred hours it measures time regularly, as registered by the movement of the hands on the face of the clock. After this period, it begins to accelerate and measure the homogeneous hour in fifty-seven minutes. The racing period continues for approximately another hundred hours after which it begins to retard in its measurement of time, and to record the standard hour in a period of fifty minutes. This phase continues for another hundred or so hours. In the next cycle, the springs of the clock begin gradually to lost their original energy and run down. For the next hundred hours, the clock increasingly retards in its measurements until it measures one half hour of time for every elapsed hour. The next one hundred hours reveals the clock as increasingly retarding until it measures a time distance of five minutes for every hour that has elapsed. Finally, within the next hundred hours, it comes to a cessation of motion. However, three hours later, the slow motion of the hands begins again. Now... when the clock came to a complete halt for a period of three hours, by what motion with reference to the rest of the physical universe do we measure it? The rest of the physical universe, was, (in the imaginative example) completely non-existent. If this is the case, can it be maintained that there is absolutely no difference between whether the motion of the clock stopped for three hours, or for one minute - or, for years? Furthermore, is there no difference between the ordinary, smooth running nature of the mechanism of the clock when it measured time regularly, and later on in the cycle when the mechanism began to fail and the clock measured the standard hour both more rapidly and more slowly by turns? This writer maintains that there is a difference and that almost all of the present audience also perceive that difference intuitively, positing that there is a difference between the clock's coming to a complete stop for three hours, etc - even if no moving objects are in existence elsewhere in the universe. This example suggests that time is more than the measure of motion. Its presence is intuit even when all standards of motion have ceased. Time must (at least in some sense to be specified later) be accorded the status of an independent existent.

Secondly, consider as an example a photographic dark room in which developing is taking place; there some motion with film is darkly visible. Now, the photographer turns the switch and no light is visible. How is the time to remain in this situation gauged: one minute, five minutes, or an hour? This demonstrates that even in the situation of a dark room (in which no real measure of motion is possible) the difference between intervals of time is recognizable. Both of the examples appear to suggest that time is not ultimately dependent upon motion: that it is not the measure of motion - but, rather an independent existent, at least to the degree in which it is independent of motion and of human cognition.

PART 4

THE IMPACT OF A REALIST SOLUTION ON EPISTEMOLOGY

Realism with reference to Time and Space provides a key to many perplexing problems in Epistemology and may well constitute the key to an effective solution to the problem of Universals; the problem of man''s knowledge of the real and the problem of Realism and Anti-realism in science. These are now considered in turn.

a) The Solution of the Problem of Universals

If space-time in the gravitational field has an independent existence; space-time is a universal, existing independently of human cognition of it. This, the position of Absolute Realism is the position that seems to have been established through the foregoing remarks. Alternative possibilities, that space-time is either a mental construct or a relationship between objects, appear to have been excluded. The position that space-time was a relationship between material objects would have established some version of "Moderate Realism" with regard to the status of Universals and the position that "space-time is a mental construct" would have established some form of either Nominalism or Conceptualism, regarding Universals.

b) The Limits of Man's Knowledge

If the space-time field is real independently of both material objects and of human cognition, then man's knowledge of the gravitational field of space-time must be equivalent to knowledge of the real world, to a knowledge of things-in-themselves, or Noumena. This assertion appears to be one of the more immediate ramifications of the position attempting to prove (through the given examples of clocks and dark rooms and expansions of standard measures) the reality of the gravitational space-time field.

Were the space-time field, conversely, proven to be merely a mental construct, a product of human cognition, either as concept or as intuiting, it would evidence that man's capacity to know the real, to apprehend the things-in-themselves, is severely limited. Were this so, the tings-in-themselves would have to be filtered through the space-time field, and man would know things only as they appear, or phenomena. Even if the space-time gravitational field were proven to be a set of relations between material objects, man's ability to know the real would be confined necessarily to understanding those relationships.

PART 5

IMPACT OF REALISM ON THE PHILOSOPHY OF SCIENCE

The Realist position in the Philosophy of Science, bases as it is on the reality of the gravitational space-time field, opens up many possible interpretations of the universe, many of them seeming metaphysical in character. For example, there is the possibility of the so-called "Many Worlds Interpretation of Quantum Mechanics", which was put forward by Spinoza in the seventeenth century. Here, it is seen that positing the reality of the space-time gravitational field could lead to the speculative possibility of a "Realistic Modal Model of the Universe".

a) The Many-Worlds Interpretation of Quantum Mechanics

Quantum Mechanics, dealing with the world of microphysical, subatomic particles, is an area of science opened up in 1900 by the physicist Max Plank, who was puzzled by the manner in which electrons emit energy, being contrary to the laws of classical physics. The levels of light radiation from so-called "black bodies" revealed that light emits energy not continuously but in small, discontinuous packets, known as the quantum of energy. The microphysical world has puzzled scientists ever since. The simultaneous behavior of light as both wave and particle is simply one expression of this puzzlement of light appearing to emit energy as both particle, with a definite quantum, and as a wave also. One of the well-known problems associated with the micro-physical world of subatomic particles evolved into what is known as the "Uncertainty Principle". The accompanying problem was that of the seeming impossibility of predicting both the position and momentum of a given subatomic particle, the electron, with equal accuracy. The Uncertainty, as formulated by Heisenberg in 1931, amounted to the claim that the uncertainty of prediction did not occur because of imperfections in faulty detection instruments, but rather in nature itself. The "Uncertainty Principle" was an important element in the so-called Copenhagen Interpretation of Quantum Mechanics.

The Copenhagen Interpretations eventually became simply one of the many interpretations of the behavior of microphysical particles which have been put forward since that time. The so-called London-Bauer Interpretation stresses the role of the observer in creating a definite position or momentum of the particle from among many possibilities. The "Many-Worlds interpretaton, on the other hand, stresses that in different and other worlds (some of which may be similar to Earth) all of the possible positions and momentums of the electron are realized, when the different worlds are taken together collectively. Therefore, what was a possible occurrence for the electron actually did take place, but in a different world, i.e., in a different region of space-time from that of planet Earth.

Consider space-time as an independent reality, which this analysis has seemingly indicated, proliferating and extending itself in many dimensions. A matrix of the behavior of three electrons in Quantum Mechanics could often describe as many as nine dimensions. Consider that the electron, which often reveals wave-like characteristics in this world, actually exhibits the behavior of a particle, with nine different positions and momentums, respectively, one of which is realized in this world, the other positions being realized in the six remaining dimensions of other possible worlds. From the perspective of the dimension of this world, the remaining worlds are simply a possibility. According to the "Many Worlds Interpretation" they exist in actuality, but in separate worlds and inaccessible to planet Earth.

The "Many Worlds Interpretation" of Quantum Mechanics is very much in line with the view of Space-Time as an independent entity. If Space-Time depends upon neither material objects nor human cognition for its existence, then there is no reason to hold that it is restricted to the three dimensions of our ordinary experience - or, even that it is somehow restricted to the four-dimensional matrix of space-time. Since the behavior of subatomic particles in quantum physics often employs more than even four dimensions, there seems to be no reason why the space-time matrix might not even proliferate in infinite numbers of dimensions, each of which are manifestations of separately existing worlds, inaccessible to man's present vantage point. This could well comprise a topic of future exploration by scientists at the frontiers of Quantum Mechanics, and the theory is based upon a Realist view of science: "The Many-Worlds Theory".

b) The Many-Modal Universe of Spinoza

Another of the possibilities created by Realist Interpretation of science may be even more challenging and fascinating to the imagination. In essence this is a modal theory of the universe, recalling the description of Reality expressed in Spinoza's famous treatise of the seventeenth century, his Ethics (1677). In Spinoza's version, only one substance, or entity, that existed on its own and was conceived through itself, was possible. There was only one "Absolute" for Spinoza in the existent universe and that was substance. The Substance manifested itself in a number of characteristics or modes, with two of which mankind is acquainted: Extension and Thought. However, substance itself was manifested in many modes, some of which mankind is simply unaware of since these modes have been placed beyond the realm of man's cognitive power. It appears that each mode is a realm of reality within itself - conceivably comparable to a separate world, beyond man's cognition. Does not the space-time matrix of Relativity and Quantum Mechanics, proliferating in so very many dimensions in scientific, physical experiments afford a quasi-empirical glimpse of separate worlds, that somehow are akin to the modes which Spinoza postulated on a philosophical basis in the seventeenth century?

CONCLUSION

REALITY AS A MANY-MODAL PLURIVERSE

It is often claimed that man lives in a universe, and in this conception, it is envisaged that the parts of the universe operate according to physical laws which are invariant and universal. The Newtonian conception of the universe, a product of science, has lent credence to the view. Is it really true? The Man-Worlds Interpretation of Quantum Mechanics, on the frontier of contemporary physics, carries with it many implications of the narrowness of this perspective. It may be that man lives in a reality comprised of many worlds, containing some striking similarity to the many existent modes inherent in the Substance Universe of Spinoza. Perhaps the future of scientific research lies in the direction of gaining a greater understanding of these many different worlds, which in a modal universe may co-exist with planet Earth. The physical laws of some of these worlds or modes may resemble this earth, but in these other worlds, or modes, the physical laws may be greatly divergent from those of Earth's.

If Philosophical Realism is correct in the Philosophy of Science,* and if the space-time matrix is a reality, not dependent on the mind or on material objects, then one of the most important ramifications of this doctrine could well be the assertion that many worlds or modes, with many different dimensions, are possible.

Consequently, man lives-not in a universe with invariant laws - but, in what Carlo Castenedas has called a pluriverse, containing many different worlds, many different modes with different physical laws in operation, different forms of knowledge and different experiences which the future of scientific investigation will unveil. An empirical, scientific method could open up these possibilities by operating under a Realistic philosophy of space-time, which, itself, is a product of empirical observation and reflection.

*This does not necessarily imply that there is no room for instrumentalist theories in science [Cf. the present author's previous work, *Scientific Knowledge Discovery of Nature or Mental Construction* (Lanham, Maryland: University Press of America, 1992)] or instrumental constructions based on three dimensional common sense. But it does imply the world of four dementsions is noumenal.

CHAPTER SEVEN

SEEDS

Ordinary garden seeds. These are some of the commonest objects in nature and packages of them can be bought in stores for a certain price. Seeds which will later develop into gardenias, azaleas, and many of our homegrown flowers if the right instructions are followed. The ordinary seeds which are found in nature seem to follow the same pattern. The acorn, with the right soil and nutrition evolves into an oak tree. Given the right soil and sunlight, seeds of various plants all develop into their fullblown, mature products, given time.

In the case of all animals with backbones, the fish, the reptiles, birds, and mammals, all life develops from a fertilized egg. Most of the physical characteristics of the fish, bird, bear, or wolf are fixed at the moment of conception. The fertilized egg from this given polar bear will develop into a polar bear, not into a moose, a lion or an oak tree. The science of genetics informs us that traits such as hair and eye color, height, basic bodily build, and sex are fixed at the moment of conception in small, threadlike structures in the egg known as chromosomes.

The chromosomes, themselves, in turn, are comprised of DNA, the scientific abbreviation of deoxyribonucleic acid, the master chemical governing the physical behavior of all life from the moment of conception. The DNA determines whether that given living thing, in the course of time, will develop into a moose, elephant, lion, wolf, or human being. It determines whether the organism will be tall or small, stout or thin. It determines whether the organism will be male or female, light or dark skinned, immediately at the moment of conception. The development of the organism unfolds in time, in the course of an entire life cycle, but all of the traits of the organism are present within the DNA instantaneously.

In the realm of nature, even the stars and galaxies of our universe seem to be involved in a life cycle which takes millions of years to unfold. All stars originate as young, hot blue stars, evolve into the middle age of our local sun as yellow stars, and finally explode as red giants, to hundreds of thousands of times their present size, finally to decay and degenerate into white dwarfs, neutron stars, and finally, black holes. Not all stars, however, necessarily follow this sequence to the end. Probably only some of them become neutron stars and black holes, as the final stages of their evolution. Whether a given star will ever eventually decay into the state of neutron star or "black hole" may heavily depend upon the original mass of the star. Only stars massive enough in the beginning will end their lives as black holes. Similarly with the universe itself. Whether the natural universe will culminate in a so-called "heat death", with only energy and no matter present, a maximum state of disorganization known as entropy, or whether it will oscillate back to its primaeval mass, thus continuing the cycle depends heavily on the original energy of the "big bang". The shape of events to come is strongly determined by that original energy.

It is almost as if the life-cycle of the stars and of the universe is regulated by a program fixed at the first moment. The evolution of the stars, for example, is governed by the critical density which is present at the star's birth, and the fate of the universe is also governed by the energy of the "big bang", as astronomers call it, which "Big Bang" took place at the birth of the universe. The fate of the stars and of the universe itself unfolds in time, but the original plan is there in an instant.

On another level, the biological level, coming back to the beginning, the fate of the life cycle of both germanium and human being are also fixed at the moment of fertilization. In the case of both of these, DNA becomes the program of life. DNA is present in the original seed. Likewise, the program of the life cycle in both star and universe are probably fixed from the first moment. The original physical reactions in both contain the "seeds" of things to come.

Historians often speak of empires which contain within themselves the "seeds" of their own future decay and dissolution. The destiny of their respective futures will unfold in time, but the "seeds" of this decay are present from the first moment. One may speak of burgeoning talent within a young child as containing the "seeds" of his own future greatness. This talent will flourish in time but the seeds are present now. In the history of ideas, also, we are familiar with the fact that certain concepts seems to lie dormant or unexpressed during a long period of gestation, suddenly take birth, germinate, mature, flourish, develop and then begin to reveal some of the signs of "old age". Newtonian physics is one example of this, the atomic theory is another, and Aristotelian philosophy is yet another. What we witness here is a phenomena which applies to abstract concepts or ideas in all fields, in science, politics, religion, and philosophy. Social institutions also, appear to undergo the same "life cycle". Tracing the history of many social institutions and concepts, it is possible to claim that they contain within themselves the "seeds" of both their own perfection and their own decay.

The dog will never produce any of the Great Ideas of the Western World. It will never grasp abstract ideas, it will never employ intelligible speech, it will never compose any symphonies, for this was not in it's "program" from the moment of conception, so these possibilities will never unfold with time. But it will always be an excellent companion for this is in it's program. Employing computer language, we could say that much depends upon the original "software" of the organism present at the moment of conception.

A given computer cannot calculate mathematical equations if this capacity is not present within the original program or "software" of the computer. The program or the "software" of any evolving entity, whether that entity be a star, the universe, a living organism, a social institution, or an idea, is, in many respects present within it from the beginning and serves the function of a "seed". One could employ the same analogy in reference to the "software" of any given computer. What a given computer can and cannot do is strongly conditioned by the original program.

What are some of the distinguishing features of a physical seed? Though the variety and the type of seeds appear to be endless, all of them appear to share certain features in common. Even ideas or social institutions may be considered to contain "seeds" in this sense. They all fix the future growth and evolution of a given thing. Often, they influence the lifespan of that given living thing or even possibly "idea". In all seeds, we can plainly discern that all of the possibilities and limitations of a given thing are present within one given time frame. In addition, the majority of seeds of all kinds, even social and psychological seeds, are not spread out in space. The "seed" contains the time and the space of future developments, but in itself, it occupies very little of either. It is usually not very large in space and its existence is often short-lived. The time and space of the "seed" is, indeed, minimal.

Yet, the "seed" generates entities which occupy, in some cases, vast stretches of both time and space. The "seed" programs future activities in time and space. Indeed, both time and space represent the division of any entity into so many parts, yet all of this future behavior somehow per-exists within the seed itself, co-ordinated, not spread out into parts.

Is it possible to speak of both the physical, and the mentalistic seed as containing within itself a program of activities in the realm of space and time which somehow itself transcends space and time, like the ordinary household recipe, which, as a form of "software", directs the production of food which does exist in space and time.

In what sense can the "seed" be said to transcend space and time?

Can the architect's blueprint transcend space and time in a similar manner and serve the function of a "seed"? Is the idea of the dimensions and shape of the desk in the mind of the carpenter a similar "seed " which transcends both time and space?

Some astronomers claim that the universe may have originated in a "black hole", the physical collapse of an ageing star into disappearance in both time and space. Perhaps the universe, with its original energies, have generated in the "program" of a "black hole", which determined in the beginning, both the initial explosion and the rate of expansion since that time. There are many astronomers who think the physical universe may be dotted with both black and white mini-holes, from which matter appears and into which it disappears. From the vantage point of our present knowledge, these could be the "seeds" of physical entities, which are distributed in time and space, although the "mini-holes" themselves occupy no space and time. Yet they program everything in space and time, in much the same manner in which seeds occupy only a small portion of space and time while yet directing the activities of everything which occupies vast portions of both time and space.

We have been conditioned to think that physical reality, sharply circumscribed within the boundaries of space and time, constitutes all of reality. If this is so, what are we to think of the architect"s blueprint, which though distributed in space and time, occupies very little of it? What of the plan in the mind of the carpenter? What are we t think of the master plan of life, DNA, which can program the long existence of the giant blue whale in such a miniscule amount of space? What of the programmed expansion of the universe, which some scientists claim exploded with exactly the requisite amount of force for the production of life? How does the existence of the mini-white and the mini-black hole fit into this thinking about space and time?

Basic reflection on a common phenomenon of nature and reality, the physical and the metaphorical "seed" plainly reveals how so much of the activity in nature and in reality was programmed from the beginning, from the moment of the entities origin or birth. It is quite true that not all the activity of any natural object or living thing is prescribed at the moment of origin since some of that activity will be a product of the environment.

Nevertheless, the program or "seed" which is present at the moment of its origin will sharply circumscribe or limit certain forms of activity. Man will never fly by the power of his own arms, and the lion will never bark like the dog. The so-called "heat death" of the universe will not occur until so many million years from now, if ever, because this was already pre-determined at the moment of the "Big Bang". Also pre-determined at the moment of the "Big Bang" were the initial conditions of the explosion which were just right for life. Initial conditions, the "seeds" could have been different.

It appears as if the plan of every natural object lies within its "seeds". And its "seeds" somehow transcend space and time. Space and time are simply parts of the whole. But the whole lay pre-existent within the plan; the idea in the mind of the carpenter of the architect, the DNA within the living organism, the mini "black" and "white" holes from which the physical universe exploded. Are these "seeds" the only visible sign which the world of nature has afforded to us of some pre-existent higher dimension, beyond time and space? Could this be the realm of those psychic ideas which we have already discussed?

CHAPTER EIGHT

THE LAST FRONTIER

The exploration of space brings us at last to those mini-black and white holes which seem to proliferate in the exterior of space. The gravitational vortex of any one of them would seem to carry with it the vast potentiality of drawing any object within its range into the so-called "singularity". The "singularity", a realm of reality in which space and time no longer exist. The gradual retardation of time and the shrinking of space to a point in which space now occupies the dimensions of a plane and in which all motion, all time has ceased to exist. Here, we encounter the "seed" from which all spatial and all temporal reality spring.

Could this seed be the psychic dimension? The realm in which all spatial and temporal reality is planned? The pre-existent realm from which all spatial and all temporal reality, all reality which is divided into distinctive parts owes its origin.

Consider the nature of a plan, a new insight or new idea. After much conscious deliberation, the new solution, the mental breakthrough occurs to you in an instant, at least in its barest outlines. Later on, you fill in the details. But the ideas as you conceive it, often occurs spontaneously and suddenly, often without any reference to physical, spatial dimensions. Suddenly, you understand how the problem in algebra, geometry, or arithmetic, or even possibly calculus can be solved. Suddenly, you decide who is the real culprit in a detective story, and you are sometimes correct. In many cases, we have abrupt flashes of insight into the nature of a person's character. Often, very suddenly, we begin to understand the meaning of a piece of contemporary music or of modern, abstract painting. And the name of the person or the past event which you have forgotten; after much prodding of the memory, instantaneously, you begin to recall everything.

Such reflections could very easily persuade one to wonder whether space and time may not be an illusion after all, or, if not an illusion, then certainly simply a reflection of the reality which is present to us in our four dimensional world.

The world of another dimension might be more complete within itself, as the world of solid geometry is somehow more complete than the world of plane geometry. In the chapter on Dimensions, this was spoken of as the realm in which we can distinguish parts which we cannot clearly separate, the psychic. Is not the world of mental reflection, the world of the psychic really like this? The intuitive idea, the mental flash or insight, is it not present in a manner which somehow transcends both time and space? We can plainly distinguish parts of the given insight but we, nevertheless, cannot separate them, for all the parts of an idea are intimately related. Again, the interrelationships of all things is one of the insights of contemporary particle physics.

THE PHILOSOPHICAL FOUNDATIONS
OF PARANORMAL PHENOMENA

It is the mind which forms all of these interrelationships, probably in a dimension which is neither spatial nor temporal. It is the mind which instantaneously sees the geometrical figures, the plot outline of the story, the rise and fall of the Roman Empire, the Paleolithic Era of the Earth's history, the entire life span of a given individual, galaxies, social forms of existence, etc.

The mind sees things in time and space. But, perhaps the Philosopher, Immanuel Kant, was right. Perhaps space and time present to us a very restricted view of things, simply a view of things-as-they appear to us. Certainly, the world appears to us in a certain way if viewed through the perspective of four dimensions. Could the mind every obtain that view of things which would be presented through the perspective of the fifth dimension?

Perhaps. Perhaps the fifth dimension is the "singularity" of the "black hole". Here, there are not separable parts, no time, and no space. Like the flash of insight, everything is present simultaneously and in one physical position. The "singularity" may be the seed, the plan from which the world as we know it originates and unfolds in space and time. The universe may be the product of consciousness, the produce of the realm of the psychic.

It is the mind which plan; it is the mind which oversees the structure of the bridge which will be built in time; it is the mind which has knowledge of the average lifespan of a given species of animal even before a given member of that species has lived out its lifespan. It is also the mind which engineers the structure of technological reality so that a given thing serves a master design or purpose. In the same way, it is the mind which designs the book, and the contents of that book, which are a product of mind, transcends both time and space. The contents of a book are not confined to the place of the individual library, keeping one copy of it. The entire contents are also present at each given instant of time. The "seeds" are present in the contents of the book; it is for each individual reader to allow those contents, those "seeds" to unfold in time and space.

The "singularity" is probably the location in the physical world of what lies, essentially beyond time and space, namely the realm of ideas, those products of the psyche which organize the physical world, while remaining beyond it. That greatest of all philosophers in the ancient world, Plato, divided the universe into the World of Ideas and the World of Matter. It was Plato, we mentioned in our first chapter, that believed that the afterlife of the soul was a return to the World of Ideas from whence it originated.

The World of Ideas, if you remember, was an imperishable world. It could not be destroyed by physical means because, like a melody, it did not consist of physical parts. Ideas such as Truth, Goodness, Beauty, Justice, and Equality cannot possibly consist of physical parts, which could be destroyed by physical means. Therefore, the World of Ideas is eternal. The World of Ideas is Immutable.

The World of Ideas, since this is not the physical, material World of Matter, does not exist in time and place. This is a mentalistic universe, which plainly transcends both space and time. This is the world in which the temporal and materialistic framework of the World of Matter participates. The soul of the true philosopher longs for the moment of death; the moment of separation of the soul from the shackles of the temporal and spatial, material body which hinders the soul in its apprehension of the World of Ideas.

True understanding comes not with the material body but with the soul. Only the intellect knows that which is eternal. Only the Intellect knows those Ideas which find no concrete embodiment in time and space. Only the Intellect contemplates pure Goodness, Truth, Beauty, Justice and Equality as they truly exist—in a world not located in space and time, i.e., in a world beyond space and time.

Ordinary intuition seems to support the idea that the concept of "Justice" must somehow be non-temporal and non-spatial in order to exist. In other words, from the perspective of ordinary intuition, when the very concept of justice appears to change with time and place, we might be tempted to claim that, in all of these cases, no one really knows what "justice" is. Many ideas appear to be quasi-mathematical. Like the mathematical constant, pi, they appear to contain within themselves an immutable character over time and space. Even ordinary ideas, ordinary insights which appear in a flash seem to share this same characteristic. The sudden insight develops within space and time though that idea, itself, appears to transcend both time and space. In a similar manner, the concepts in the World of Ideas are like "seeds" which transcend both time and space, and later find development within space and time. The idea of the desk in the mind of the carpenter will find development within space and time.

Might Plato's ancient World of Ideas be what some contemporary physicists refer to as the "singularity"? Let us assume that the "singularity" is the "seed" from which the physical universe unfolds in space and time. The "seed" contains the "idea", according to which the entity will develop, both spatially and temporally.

The origin of the universe itself or what astronomers refer to as the "Big Bang", may be owing to just such a "singularity". Beyond space and time, this "singularity" contains the intellectual, designed conscious instruction, directing the universe to expand at a given rate, a rate neither too fast nor too slow for the appearance of life. This may be the best explanation for what has long puzzled a few scientists, the so-called Anthropic Principle, or the apparent suitability of physical conditions of the eventual evolution of both life and man.

CHAPTER NINE

ATOMS AND EIDOS: THE EMERGING CONTEMPORARY PHILOSOPHY

In the ancient world, the philosopher, Democritus of Abdera, arrived at the theory that reality was constituted by particles too small to be seen with the human eye. It was one of several ancient theories which attempted to solve the problem of the one and the many. If reality is comprised of many thing, how is it possible for anything, living or non-living, animal or man, to change and yet to remain the same animal or man?

The only explanation the philosophers of this era could employ to account for change was in terms of some underlying unity. Before Democritus, philosophers such as Thales, Anaximander, Anaximines, Parmenides and Zeno had all attempted to reduce reality to one thing, either one quantity or one quality. The problem confronting philosophers such as Parmenides was how, if everything, in ultimate reality was one, could any motion or change take place in the universe?

There have been basically two enduring solutions to this problem of change in ancient Greek philosophy. One tactic is to claim that reality is ultimately pluralistic or, rather, comprised of many things which fit into different sorts or categories. These basic elements of nature change, it is claimed, because they move about in a void. Another tactic is to claim that reality is ultimately dualistic, or comprised of two things, changeless forms, or ideas, and changing matter. It was the first of these tactics which inspired Democritus, who claimed that all of nature consisted of atoms, hard particles too small to be seen with the human eye, and the void, or, the empty space in which they moved. For Democritus, things changed because atoms moved in the void. The second tactic was adapted, essentially by Plato. The World of Ideas never changed, but the World of Matter, which participated in the Ideas was subject to change.

The idea of Form of a given thing in the World of Ideas was its eidos, its enduring structure. For Plato's pupil, the great philosopher, Aristotle, things were known through their eidos, their form, their permanent structure. Matter changed, but the form did not. For Aristotle, the eidos of man consisted in his rational nature, and it was this eidos which was the permanent or underlying structure in all those non-essential or accidental changes of height, weight, shape, clothing, geographical location, etc., which the rational being underwent throughout the course of a lifetime. For Aristotle, the eidos did not exist independently of man in a World of Ideas but was embedded in man himself.

It is, nevertheless, the case that for both Plato and Aristotle the form was the underlying changeless principle which mad a thing to be the kind of thing it was. Things were known through their eidos, whether that eidos was conceived of as separately existing or as embodies within the thing. The eidos was the changeless essence of nature of a given thing.

By way of contrast, for Democritus, there was no eidos. Things were simply comprised of atoms in motion throughout the void. The atoms comprising the soul in man were smooth and round and fiery. They occupied both space and time. In the final analysis, they were material. For Democritus, the human person was simply a different conglomeration of atoms, all of which were material.

For Democritus, man possessed no immaterial eidos or rational nature which was not somehow reduceable to atoms in motion. The same] was true of all realities which we saw before us in nature..They were all reduceable to atoms moving throughout a vast void. How many champions Democritus has, even with the advent of twentieth century physics. Many physicists and biologists reduce material, nature, animals and man to matter in motion.

All physical objects are analyzed, through sophisticated scientific equipment, to the smallest elements of which they are comprised, the atoms. And all atoms are material. What is forgotten in the process of this analysis is the total, embracing structure, the eidos. Modern physics, i.e., the physics before the advent of Einstein and quantum physics knows only the matter of atoms moving about in a void or in space. Twentieth century physics, again, according to Capek, teach us better. We now challenge ordinary experience with more intensity. We know that space, time, matter, and motion have no clear boundaries. Nature itself, challenges our everyday concepts of space, time, matter, and motion whenever they are reminded of the Einstein-Podalsky-Rosen experiment which we have discussed previously. Reality transcends ordinary, atomistic, concepts of space, time, motion, and matter, as separate atomic units.

The understanding of nature now, in our twentieth century, requires that we grasp not as a conglomeration of discrete atoms but rather as a whole. We must understand the entire structure; we must understand the eidos of a given thing. In regard to psychic phenomena, we cannot understand this phenomena of nature atomistically. Atomistic understanding is limited in the fact of such mysterious activity as the manipulation of objects at a distance and the paired behavior of sub-atomic particles many miles away. The atomistic understanding of the human person is not adequate to deal with out-of the body experience, teleportation, the so-called dual personality, the possibility of one mind controlling more than one body, psychokinesis, or many other cases in which mind seems to prevail over matter..It is too prosaic, dull, and completely unimaginative for these possibilities.

Let us consign it to its grave for it has long outlived its usefulness. In its stead, the ancient doctrine of the eidos might serve us better. This, at least, was an attempt to see reality whole, to grasp the entire structure of a thing. The eidos is not necessarily to be identified with its time and place, which is often simply an accidental manifestation of it. Hence,the eidos could manifest itself in two or more places at once. The eidos could teleport, it could co-habit one body with the eidos of one not identical with this, it could manipulate objects at a distance because in some sense it transcends both space and time.

The mechanistic philosophy of matter, motion, space and time is dead, and with that, atomism. It was all too simple-minded. It never challenged ordinary, commonsensical ideas. Let us leave it to the nineteenth century, where it belongs. A revival of another old tradition, that of the eidos, because of its greater sophistication and because it challenges the imagination more vigorously, could answer many presently unsolvable puzzles in the realm of physic phenomena. The empirical evidence for the existence of these phenomena is overwhelming; it is simply a matter of changing our worldview.

ANNOTATED BIBLIOGRAPHY

GENERAL INTRODUCTIONS

Heaps, Willard A. Psychic Phenomena. New York: Thomas Nelson, Inc., 1974. This book covers many areas of parapsychology, and includes a good treatment of psychokinesis.

Rhine, Dr. Joseph Banks. Extra-Sensory Perception. Boston: Branden Press, 1964. A synopsis of research in Duke University and elsewhere, by the director of the parapsychology laboratory in Duke.

Philosophical

Broad, Charlie Dunbar. Lectures on Psychical Research. New York: Humanities Press, 1962. Well documented.

Religion, Philosophy, and Psychical Research. New York: Humanities Press, 1969. (First Published, 1953.) Especially of interest is the chapter entitled "The Relevance of Psychical Research to Philosophy". This chapter consists of a discussion of what Broad calls, the Limiting Principles governing psychic research. These are general principles which, in Broad's opinion, are fundamental to Western Philosophy. Only by questioning these principles does psychic research become plausible. Broad's treatment dovetails, in some respects, with the treatment of this report.

Ducasse, Curt John. The Belief in a Life after Death. Springfield, Illinois: Charles C. Thomas, 1961. A philosophical treatment of the empirical evidence of the mind's continues existence after death.

Koestler, Arthur. The Roots of Coincidence: An Excursion into Parapsychology. New York: Random House, 1972. One of the best in-depth accounts of the philosophical implications of paranormal phenomena which has been written to date. The author relates psychic phenomena to contemporary physics, stressing, at least to some extent, the Principle of Complementarity. Deals with some interesting relationships not mentioned in this report.

Specific Areas

Psychokinesis

Rhine, Louisa E. Mind Over Matter: Psychokinesis. New York: MacMillan Co., 1970. A very detailed treatment of this topic by the wife of Dr. Joseph Banks Rhine. Also a professor at Duke University with her husband.

Teleportation

Monroe, Robert A. Journeys out of the Body. Garden City, N.Y.: Doubleday, 1973. Probably the most detailed account of this topic in existence.

Of Related Interest

Capek, Milec. The Philosophic impact of Contemporary Physics. Princeton, N.J.: D. van Nostrand Co., 1961. Capek explicates and expounds upon the changes in conceptual framework from nineteenth century to twentieth century science.

Coleman, James. A. Relativity for the Layman: A Simplified Account of the History, Theory, and Proofs of Relativity. New York: New American Library, 1958. Highly recommended by no less than Einstein himself.

Prosch, Harry. The Genesis of 20th Century Philosophy: The Evolution of Thought from Copernicus to the Present. New York: Thomas Y. Crowell Co., 1964. Describes and explains many of the important themes which became dominant in philosophy from the time of the Renaissance onward. An outstanding analysis of the meaning of modern and contemporary philosophy.

FOOTNOTES

1. See C. Howard Hinton. A New Era of Thought (London: Swann Sonnenschein & Co., 1888)

2. See P.D. Ouspensky's Tertium Organum (New York: Random House, 1970) 1st Published by Manas Press, 1920)

3. James A. Coleman, Relativity for the Layman: A Simplified Account of the History, Theory and Proofs of Relativity, pp. 32-37.

4 .Op. cit., pp. 40-42.

5. Op. cit., pp. 44-91.

6. Op. cit., pp. 92-108.

7. Op. cit., pp. 120-124.

8. Cf. Gary Zukav, The Dancing Wu Li Masters: An Overview of the New Physics. (New York: Bantam Books, 1980.) pp. 285-293

Contains description of the Einstein-Podolsky-Rosen Experiment.

Remainder of the chapter, pp. 293-317 for a recounting of three different interpretations of the experiment. This experiment dealing with the behavior of sub-atomic particles was first performed in 1935. It revealed an unsuspected correlation in both the spin and direction of similar particles over vast distances, too vast to be connected by signals, since the signals would have to travel faster than the speed of light. All three of the theories were designed to explain this effect that postulates an underlying interconnectedness within Nature. The Superluminal Connections Theory amounts to the statement that information is communicated between one physical space and another instantaneously, because the transfer takes place in a region beyond space and time. The Man-Worlds Theory claims that different possible modes of reality co-exist simultaneously and that they are all internally correlated. According to the theory of Super-determinism, all subatomic particles are correlated, and the physical universe could not exist otherwise than it is.

9. See: Milec Capek, The Philosophic Impact of Contemporary Physics, Especially relevant here is the conclusion.

10. See: Carol White. Energy Potential: Toward a New Electromagnetic Field Theory, (N.Y.: Campaigner Publications, 1977.)

Also: Robert A. Coleman, op. cit., p. 122.

1. See: Milec Capek, Op. Cit., especially the conclusion.

2. See: James A. Coleman Op. cit., p. 122.

3. See: Willard A. Heaps, Psychic Phenomena. pp. 11-113 and the entire Chapter 6.

14. See Op. cit., pp. 95-99 and the entire Chapter 5.

15. See Op. cit., pp. 123 and the entire Chapter 7.

16. See Op. cit., pp. 139-142. Especially p. 139.

17. See Op. cit., pp. 167-168.

18. See Op. cit., pp. 140-141.

19. See Op. cit., pp. 153-156.

20. See Op. cit., p. 143 and the entire Chapter 8.

21. See: Bibliography

22. Alfred North Whitehead, Science and the Modern World, Chapter III and Process and Reality, pp. 159-160.